BIG HELP

for Small Youth Groups

Compiled by Richard Ross

Convention Press
Nashville, Tennessee

2

This book is the text for course number 23-071 in the subject area Pastoral Ministries of
the Church Study Course

Dewey Decimal Classification: 259.23

Subject Heading: CHURCH WORK WITH YOUTH // YOUTH MINISTRY
Printed in the United States of America

Church Administration Department
Sunday School Board, SBC
127 Ninth Avenue, North
Nashville, Tennessee

This books is dedicated to William (Bill) Cromer. Dr. Cromer has been a full-time member of the faculty at Southern Baptist Theological Seminary since 1961. His teaching areas have included youth education and youth ministry. Over a period of 30 years, he has touched the lives of hundreds of students now serving in youth-related positions.

Bill Cromer has consistently demonstrated a love for teenagers in smaller churches. Both through his own ministry and through the lives of his students, he has made a rich contribution to Southern Baptist youth ministry.

Contents

4

Chapter One

Ministering to Youth in Small Churches

William R. Cromer, Jr.

William R. Cromer, Jr. is professor of Christian education, Southern Baptist Theological Seminary, Louisville, Kentucky.

Use your imagination and think about what youth ministry was like in the early church. You can't? Why? Could it be because we know so little about it? And which of the apostles can you see as the youth leader? Aggressive Peter? Practical James? Thomas, the researcher, wanting empirical evidence?

We may not be able to imagine this situation, but we can be fairly certain that youth groups in the early church were small, because the churches were new and small even when located in the cities of the Bible. Emphasis on small youth groups is thus compatible with the pattern of most New Testament churches.

6

Small Is Historical

At the time of the Civil War, the average Protestant church in America had fewer than 100 members. By 1900, the average was still less than 150 members. The few large churches were located in the center of a city or in ethnic communities.[1]

When the Southern Baptist Convention was organized in 1845, it reported 352,950 members and a Sunday School enrollment of 78,900.[2] The statistically average church had 65 enrolled in Sunday School. In 1891, the statistically average church in the SBC had 58 enrolled in Sunday School.[3]

In 1986, the statistically average Southern Baptist church had 220 enrolled in Sunday School with 285 resident members and reported 12 baptisms.[4] In 1987, 80 percent of all SBC churches had fewer than 400 members. Only 7.8 percent had one thousand or more total members.[5]

Such statistics strongly suggest that America is not a nation of predominantly large churches. In fact, in 1987, the median Southern Baptist church had 239 total and 171 resident members.[6] Most church youth groups are, therefore, small to moderate size, including those in the SBC.

Beyond emphasizing the essentially small nature of most SBC churches and youth groups, this chapter will examine some needs of small groups and explore certain advantages.

> **SBCFACT: Approximately the same number of SBC churches are in rural areas today as 40 years ago. In 1949, there were 22,877; in 1988, 22,060 (59%).[7]**

Small Youth Groups Have Special Needs

Just as in large groups, small church youth groups help meet developmental needs common to all youth. For example, all youth must adjust to the physiological changes of puberty and growing into young adulthood. Finding both acceptance and distance in peer relationships, achieving appropriate sex roles, exploring occupational choices, adopting a moral-ethical code for living, and coping acceptably with authority are other needs common to adolescents.

New needs.—The past 20 years or so have also created a new set of problems and needs for youth, parents, and leaders.

Drugs have become the scourge of American society, leaving addiction, crime, violence, and degradation in their wake. Teen suicides have increased dramatically. Alcohol, the socially approved drug of choice, is claiming young lives to alcoholism and automobile accidents. A 1986 study of 650 seventh and eighth graders in a small town and its surrounding area found that 88 percent reported having had at least one drink during the past 12 months. Sixty-five percent of youth who attended church began drinking by age 13.[8] Small youth groups cannot escape these problems.

Teen pregnancies are epidemic. Sexual promiscuity is spreading disease at alarming rates. AIDS is a lurking threat in every boy-girl relationship. Teenage illiteracy has produced 27 million illiterate adults, and an additional 35 million American adults are functionally illiterate (unable to cope with the demands of daily living).[9] Add to this incomplete litany the hidden crimes of sexual, physical, and psychological abuse; and consider that all of these needs confront small, as well as large, churches and their leaders.

Small group needs.—Membership in a small youth group can generate certain other needs which are endemic to the life of the group itself. One such need is for sensitive adults who guide and help youth develop leadership skills. Many youth experience their first real chance to stand and speak, lead in prayer, or to serve in a leadership role through their church youth group. Youth participation and leadership are probably made more necessary and possible in smaller groups.

Involvement in denominational meetings at associational, state, and convention-wide levels is especially important for small youth groups. Such experiences can produce a broader conception of youth ministry, facilitate identification with a larger fellowship of Christians, and create occasions for personal response to a broader range of Christ's claims upon life. Anyone who has ever been present at a commissioning service for denominational missionaries has heard testimonies to the influence of such experiences. Church can thereby become more to youth than social activity, parochial concerns, or minimal involvement.

8

> **SBCFACT: Slightly over 69 percent of the smallest churches (under 50) and 90 percent of those with 150-199 members have both morning and evening services each Sunday.[10]**

Competent, responsible, committed adult leaders are even more essential when the youth group is small. One or two absent, chronic late-arrivers, or unprepared leaders can destroy a Sunday School lesson or youth presentation. Some leaders feel that "our small group" does not need as much planning or guidance as do larger groups. And lay leaders are even more crucial when a church has no employed youth staff member as a resource person. Richard Ross reports that about 8,000 churches have employed youth ministers, but perhaps 15,000 have volunteer youth leaders.

Certain activities and experiences can exceed the financial or membership size of small groups. When this is the case, leaders should consider collaborating with a larger youth group in activities such as extended mission trips, a church-sponsored Christian music concert, or extensive mission action projects. Larger groups will often welcome a chance to help smaller groups.

A commendable example for meeting this need was the initiative taken by Gene Johnson, minister of youth at Hermitage Hills Baptist Church, Hermitage, Tennessee. His youth sponsored Goofy Olympics for all church youth in their area. Fourteen events were included. Each youth group paid for its own members, enabling small youth groups to enjoy what might otherwise have been inaccessible.

> **SBCFACT: Churches with fewer than one hundred members had a higher per capita giving average ($284) than the average for all SBC churches ($279) in 1988.[11]**

Have you ever met anyone with an "ensmallment" mentality? Small youth group members may become infected with this virus which blames group size for things such as membership stagnation, inadequate programs, and scarce creativity. One antidote for this is to enable youth to feel that "in all these things we are more than conquerors through him that loved us" (Rom. 8:37). Just as missions are never foreign, from God's perspective no youth groups are really small. However, sometimes "small churches lack intentionality about the church's life and work."[12] Low group-esteem causes members to concentrate on survival rather than pursue ministry opportunities.

Small youth groups resemble other small groups more than they do larger youth groups. One similarity of small groups is a temptation to protect their group identity by erecting invisible barriers to membership. These appear in unwritten and even unspoken rules which dictate belonging, acceptance, and genuine inclusion in the group. Cliques develop and newcomers, despairing of ever feeling like "one of us," may become dropouts.

Small youth groups probably must work even harder than others to balance strong group identity with positive efforts to include prospects, visitors, and newcomers. Small churches are difficult to enter and almost impossible to kill.[13]

> **SBCFACT: Youth baptisms totaled 80,391 in 1988 or 23.3 percent of the SBC total.[14]**

Small Is Beautiful

All sizes of youth groups have limitations and advantages. For example, large groups have staff leaders as resource persons, adequate budget support, a large pool of potential youth leaders, and are able to attend distant youth program events (even overseas). Large youth groups often have attractive facilities, community recognition and participation, strong musical opportunities, recreational facilities, and countless other assets.

However, being small also has assets. English writer E. F. Schumacher's 1973 book was titled *Small is Beautiful.* His thesis was that people are so enamored with bigness that they fail to adequately see the need and value of the small and simple in their world. He applied his theme to the survival of "Space Ship Earth" and subtitled his work *Economics as if People Mattered.*[15]

Remember the seal which malfunctioned and caused the space shuttle disaster; the business-card-sized, metal repair plates purchased by the U. S. Air Force in 1989 for its C-5 cargo planes at a cost of $114 each; or Britain's crown jewels in England's Tower of London? Surely everyone would acknowledge these as examples of "small is beautiful" and valuable, especially if people matter.

To identify some strengths of small youth groups in no way diminishes the values of larger groups or implies that these are unique to small groups. But small churches and groups have been described as "disorganized, uncommitted, and afraid of change," reports Carl Dudley.[16] So in a constructive spirit some virtues of small youth groups need to be identified.

> **SBCFACT: Seventy-eight percent of SBC churches have fewer than 500 members.[17]**

Family identity.—Youth in small groups tend to be identified with their family, in whatever configuration and degree of church involvement their family represents. These relationships facilitate recognition and support of peers and adults.

In our youth group at West Little River Baptist Church (now 79th Street) in Miami, Florida, I always felt I was viewed as an important and significant person. My parents were active church members, and I was known as their son and youngest to my two older brothers. Sometimes I suspect certain of my fits of better behavior were aided by that recognition. Family identity is a common experience in a small youth group.

Leadership training.—Leaders of small youth groups are often well trained and prepared for their ministry. Many have a strong feeling of responsibility and are open to experiences which help them function more adequately. They, therefore, often participate in associational and regional training events, including Ridgecrest and Glorieta programs.

Youth leader and deacon Audrey Bryant of Ridgecrest Baptist Church in North Carolina attended, with her son David, the Baptist Youth World Conference in South America and in Glasgow, Scotland. They will participate in an evangelistic mission in Brazil and already plan to be present for the next world youth conference scheduled for Africa! Some of the best youth leaders minister through small youth groups.

Service opportunities.—Opportunities to use talents and develop personal gifts are accessible to all youth in small groups.

To lead in prayer, give a testimony, usher, sing (even with a less than perfect voice) a musical solo, or play a simple hymn on Sunday night without being markedly skilled can be options for youth in small groups. Small groups often show as much genuine appreciation for willing effort as for skill and proficiency.

Persons are also permitted the right to fail with minimal risk of embarrassment or humiliation. Appreciation and encouragement can outweigh failures or limited skills.

Parents.—Parental concern for youth has increased markedly. Aware of some youth needs and problems, parents are becoming more willing to learn better parenting skills. Small youth groups can interact with parents and create trust which improves communication between individual youth and their parents.

Donna Turner found advantage in her group of fewer than 15 at Jefferson Park Baptist Church in Charlottesville, Virginia. The entire group was able to meet in a different home each week for Bible study. Being "at home" helped parents "to see what we did during Bible study. Many times the youth were an inspiration to the adults. Parent-youth communication increased, relationships grew, and bonds were renewed."

Pastor as friend.—Several years ago students in one of my classes surveyed youth in three Louisville churches. Of the 55 respondents, 45 percent said they knew their pastor well and 18 percent said they knew him very well. The remaining 40 percent wanted their pastor to be a friend. Almost all of those who said they knew their pastor little or not at all were from the large suburban church in the sample.

Face-to-face interactions can build feelings of trust and friendship between the pastor and youth. While the personality and temperament of the pastor and other youth leaders are crucial factors, consistent contacts create bridges for ministry when difficulties and needs arise in the lives of youth and their families. One of the best human gifts youth can receive is a pastor who is "my friend."

Hurting and caring.—Hurting and hiding in a small group is usually difficult. Absence, a change of expression or attitude, withdrawal, or even sitting in a different pew will be more quickly noticed by members of a small group.

One Sunday I asked a fellow church member, "How are you today?"

12

"I'm mad," she replied. "Someone sat in my seat this morning, and I'm going home!"

She left before the worship service began. While her behavior was not commendable, her ownership of certain space on a pew illustrates an important point for understanding people in churches.

Observant leaders know that people are placed in the physical and activity structures of a group, especially in a small congregation or group. One technique for studying this sociogram is called the choreography of worship. Draw a diagram of the sanctuary with pews, pulpit, choir, etc. Mark where you usually sit in the diagram and put initials where others whom you know sit. Circle the initials of those to whom you usually speak on Sundays. Recognize that you have placed them—as they have placed themselves—in both the physical and worship structures of the church. Consider now how aware you are of the expressions, words, and appearance of these persons and how increased is the likelihood that you would recognize that they are hurting and attempt to provide caring. One pastor described his conversation with a church member while sitting in a pew as "listening to the pew."[18]

John Powell said that all persons need a "place where their absence would be felt and their death mourned."[19] Small youth groups can provide that feeling of community and being at home by becoming a place where God can become flesh and dwell among us (see John 1:14).

> **SBCFACT: In small Sunday Schools teachers are more likely to have personal knowledge of group members attending than is the case in larger churches.[20]**

Need-driven programs.—Lawrence Richards warns that larger youth groups tend to provide programs which have been selected and shaped by only a representative group of youth, e.g., Youth Ministry Council, youth committee, etc.[21] Small groups tend to function as a committee of the whole. Needs can be more directly met when programs are shaped by all members.

Of course, programs might be shaped by an even smaller core group of youth who are the most influential. Further, the needs which are supposed to generate programs may be restricted to interests of the moment, omitting needs of which youth may presently be unaware, e.g., self-sacrifice, conserving earth's resources, world peace, hunger, etc. As Glenn Ludwig cautions, "Well, what do you want to do?" is the wrong question to ask youth because they do not know the answer. The approach is too easy and superficial. It reflects a "do something" approach, and, most importantly, it deals with wants and not needs.[22]

SBCFACT: Small churches lack intentionality about the church's life and work.[23]

Opportunities for leadership.—Every youth wants to have an important role in the peer group, wants to make the team. Small groups make it a little less likely that a few elected or vocal youth will always dominate group affairs. Members with lesser skills can have a better chance of getting to do, experience, learn, and grow than in a larger church or group. Programs and activities simply require a higher percentage of member involvement if they are to succeed. Therefore, more incentive exists to woo and encourage members to make a speech, lead a committee, or help plan a program. In small groups you can make the team without being the most attractive, talented, or charming.

Extensive research has identified two types of group belonging.[24] Membership groups are those in which belonging is based more on the meaning of the group to others and the effect belonging has on nonmembers. Group involvement does not tend to shape attitudes and behaviors when members are apart from the group. Reference groups, however, are based on what happens in and through the group itself and become a source of value choices, beliefs, and guidance for behavior. Small youth groups appear to show more than average promise for serving as true reference groups for their members.

SBCFACT: Small churches are groups in which "How are you?" is a question not a greeting.[25]

14

Uniform school identity.—One minister of youth in a large metropolitan area reported that the different middle and high schools attended by their church youth totaled 53. Imagine a youth group with such diverse experiences, identities, time commitments, and loyalties. While this may add richness and more programming ideas, it also adds complexity for leaders seeking to relate to youth in terms of their schools whose 35 or more hours of weekly influence is enormous.

Members of smaller groups are likely to be pupils in a smaller number of schools and, in some churches, to represent no more than two or three. This enables them to be more identified with their community, immediate neighborhood, and church. Fewer schools simplify the task of programming for youth and decrease conflicts with school schedules. Participation of youth leaders in school events in which youth are involved is facilitated, an important presence for both youth and their families. Outreach to other school youth is also easier.

Witnessing.—Youth leaders must be committed to winning youth to personal faith in Christ and to helping them grow in discipleship. The intimate contact and interaction within small groups can help leaders feel comfortable and confident in this witnessing ministry. Small congregations usually provide concern and support for the evangelism of youth.

> **SBCFACT: In 1988, Youth Sunday School enrollment was 1,055,999 which was 13.3 percent of the SBC total but was down .4 percent from 1987. Most people are won to Christ through the Sunday School.** [26]

Is a Book for Small Youth Groups Needed?

Why is a book like this one needed? Three reasons are suggested.

Most of the history of American church life has been characterized by efforts to develop curricula, programs, and strategies which could be applied equally to all size churches.—Small churches were counseled to adapt the suggestions to their special circumstances. Two examples of this were the International Uniform Sunday School Lesson Series (begun in 1872) and the Standard Sunday School Guide, the latter developed by

Southern Baptists. Both were originally intended for churches of all sizes and types. Only later were they changed to meet needs of smaller churches, and often such changes in materials came only when they were demanded by the smaller churches.

This text is a logical part of a continuing trend among Southern Baptists to respond more helpfully to the needs of smaller churches, in this case, the needs of smaller youth groups.—Specific evidences of this trend are to be found in books such as *The Small Sunday School at Work, Helping a Small Church Grow,* and *Small Sunday School Director's Guide*, all available through the Baptist Sunday School Board.

Further evidence of such efforts is seen in the helps for small churches in *Sunday School Leadership* magazine, the expansion and undergirding of bivocational pastorates, and the newly adopted program of a "field of churches" in which several churches are served by the same pastor—an admitted return to the circuit-riding-preacher pattern of an earlier era.

It represents the first resource of its kind produced by Southern Baptists for ministry in small youth groups.—It is a historically significant volume. For the first time the experience and insights of experts in youth ministry are focused on the needs of small youth groups and their leaders, whether paid or volunteer. This unique contribution should provide much needed help for small youth groups.

> **SBCFACT: About half of SBC churches with fewer than 150 members have a bivocational pastor (9,170 in 1987).[27]**

Small groups of "citizens of the Kingdom" were called by the 18th-century British statesman Edmund Burke the "little platoons" of God who make a difference through their works of justice, mercy, and charity.[28] This book is written in the hope that it will be used of God as a new tool to enable small church youth groups to function increasingly as God's "little platoons" in all their places of influence.

---

[1]*Membership Trends in the United Presbyterian Church in the USA* (General Assembly Mission Council, United Presbyterian Church, USA, 1976), 81 as cited in Carl S. Dudley, *Making the Small Church Effective* (Nashville: Abingdon, 1978), 23.

16

[2]P. E. Burroughs, *The Story of the Sunday School Board of the Southern Baptist Convention* (Nashville: Sunday School Board of the SBC, 1931), 18.

[3]E. P. Alldredge, "Progress of Southern Baptist Sunday Schools," *The Quarterly Review* 5.3 (July-August-September 1945): 10-14.

[4]"Southern Baptist Highlights," *The Quarterly Review* 47.4 (July-August-September 1987): 29.

[5]*Update*, Research Division of the Home Mission Board, vol. 10, no. 8, September 1988.

[6]Ibid.

[7]James A. Lowry, "Selected SBC Trends," *The Quarterly Review* 49.3 (April-May-June 1989): 52.

[8]Stephen Gibbons, Mary Lou Wylie, et al., "Patterns of Alcohol Use Among Rural and Small-Town Adolescents," *Adolescence*, Winter 1986, 887-900.

[9]*Common Focus*, Center for Early Adolescence, University of North Carolina at Chapel Hill, vol. 8, no. 1, 1987, 1.

[10]Martin Bradley, "Speaking of Statistics," The Quarterly Review 49.3 (April-May-June 1989): 62.

[11]"Southern Baptist Highlights," *The Quarterly Review* 49.4 (July-August-September 1989): 49.

[12]Generalization from various sources in *Small Churches in the Southern Baptist Convention*, C. Kirk Hadaway, December 1986, Baptist Sunday School Board, 6.

[13]Ibid.

[14]"Southern Baptist Highlights," *The Quarterly Review* 49.4 (July-August-September 1989): 21.

[15]E. F. Schumacher, *Small Is Beautiful* (New York: Harper and Row, 1973).

[16]Dudley, 14.

[17]"Southern Baptist Highlights," *The Quarterly Review* 49.4 (July-August-September 1989): 23.

[18]Dudley, *Making the Small Church Effective*, 31.

[19]John Powell, *Fully Human, Fully Alive* (Niles, IL: Argus Communications, 1976), 27.

[20]Brooks Faulkner, et. al., "A Look at the Small Church—a Survey of Small Churches in the SBC" (Nashville: Baptist Sunday School Board, 1970).

[21]Lawrence Richards, *Youth Ministry*, rev. ed. (Grand Rapids, MI: Zondervan Publishing House, 1985). 285-91.

[22]Glenn Ludwig, *Building an Effective Youth Ministry* (Nashville: Abingdon Press, 1979), 19-26.

[23]Hadaway, *Small Churches*, 6.

[24]Muzafer Sherif, 0. J. Harvey, et. al., *Intergroup Conflict* (Norman, OK: University of Oklahoma, 1961). Additional research was reported in later articles by Muzafer and Carolyn Sherif and others.

[25]Hadaway, *Small Churches*, 6.

[26] "Southern Baptist Highlights," *The Quarterly Review* 49.4 (July-August-September 1989): 33.

[27]*The Quarterly Review* 49.3 (April-May-June 1989): 55.

[28]Quoted in George F. Will, *Statescraft and Soulcraft: What Government Does* (New York: Simon and Schuster, 1983), 129.

Personal Learning Activities

1. In what ways are small youth groups unique?

2. What are the relative strengths and weaknesses for youth of small churches?

3. What steps can small churches take to overcome some of their limitations in ministry to youth?

Chapter Two

Being an Effective Youth Ministry Coordinator

Richard Ross

Richard Ross is youth ministry consultant, Church Administration Department, Sunday School Board, Nashville, Tennessee.

What would happen if a great orchestras tried to perform a thrilling symphony with no conductor? What if each musician just began playing at some point after the curtain rose? What if trombonists still oiling their slides were caught off guard by impatient piccolos who had already begun? What if the violins thought a passage should be played much slower than the oboes thought it should?

Clearly the concert would be a frustrating experience. Even though the orchestra is composed of gifted musicians, their talents would be lost without a conductor. Someone has to blend the talents of many into a unified whole.

Church youth ministries also need a conductor. Each congregation needs someone who can blend the gifts and energy of others into a balanced, comprehensive ministry with youth.

The Position
Every congregation with youth in grades 7 through 12 should have a designated youth ministry coordinator. A variety of people might fill that role.

In some churches the pastor may fill this position. In addition to his churchwide ministry, he may also tie together all that the church is doing with and for youth, youth workers, and parents of youth.

In other churches a staff member may have other staff assignments in addition to serving as a youth ministry coordinator. Possible titles include minister of music and youth, minister of education and youth, minister of youth and recreation.

In still other churches a committed volunteer serves as youth ministry coordinator. He or she gives full attention to orchestrating the church's various programs and ministry with youth, youth workers, and parents of youth. In some churches a married couple share the position.

The majority of volunteer youth ministry coordinators have direct teaching responsibilities in addition to their coordination role. For example, a youth ministry coordinator may also serve as a Youth Sunday School teacher or Acteen leader. Ideally, a youth ministry coordinator should be able to give full attention to guiding the church's total ministry to youth. Realistically, though, most coordinators fill teaching positions when too few leaders are available.

Paid youth ministry coordinators often have the title *minister of youth* or one of the combination titles listed above. Some volunteer youth ministry coordinators also have the title *minister of youth*. They perceive themselves as members of the church's ministerial staff.

Other volunteers feel comfortable with titles such as *youth ministry coordinator, youth director,* or *youth chairperson.* They realize they occupy a vital church leadership position, but they do not see themselves as members of the ministerial staff. The title *youth ministry coordinator* is growing in popularity and is most descriptive of this position.

20

The Need

A church with youth needs a youth ministry coordinator more than an orchestra needs a conductor. Consider these factors.

Every youth program needs someone who sees the big picture.—Every church should be grateful for workers who teach youth. They make a valuable contribution. However, the church cannot expect a Youth Discipleship leader to follow closely what is being done in youth missions education, nor can the church expect a faithful sponsor of youth activities to know all that is happening in Youth Sunday School.

Someone needs to step back from the sounds of clarinets and bassoons to listen to the overall performance. A youth ministry coordinator is in a position to ask questions such as these: Is our present youth program appealing only to youth with an interest in sports? Why don't the junior-high girls who come on Wednesday nights also come on Sunday mornings? Do we need to shift more of our emphasis this year to discipleship experiences for teenagers?

Every youth program needs someone to provide motivation.— Church members who care about teenagers may or may not be making a contribution to those youth. The lives of most adults are complicated and busy. Members with good intentions may allow other activities to come before working with youth.

Effective youth ministry coordinators provide a spark of excitement that motivates others to make a contribution. Their own initiative and spirit become a focal point that results in others' wanting to get involved.

Every youth program needs someone to relate to the church staff or Church Council.—The youth program should be closely tied to the ongoing life of the church. The youth program should fit well with the overall plans the staff and Church Council have for the church. The youth ministry coordinator is in the best position to see that this happens.

Every youth program needs someone to guide the work of the Youth Ministry Council.—A growing number of churches use a team approach to planning and implementing the youth program. A Youth Ministry Council—composed of representative youth, youth workers, and parents of youth—gives overall direction to youth ministry. To be effective a Youth Ministry Council needs a leader. The youth ministry coordinator is the ideal choice.

Every youth program needs someone to plan and administer a youth budget.—Whether a church has a large budget or a small one, someone needs to prepare a budget proposal and then administer how that money is spent during the year. The youth ministry coordinator is the logical choice.

Every youth program needs someone who gives visibility to the church's work with youth, youth workers, and parents.—Here is a startling thought. Every church with at least one youth has a youth program. This is true because everything a church does with and for teenagers is part of the youth program. Sunday morning Bible study *is* the youth program. Sunday morning worship *is* the youth program.

A church has a youth program even before calling or enlisting its first youth ministry coordinator. Identifying a person in this special role, though, does heighten the visibility of the youth program. Filling this position says to youth, youth families, and the general membership that work with teenagers is a high priority for the church.

Philosophy of Ministry
Most orchestra performances include several musical selections. The conductor announces to the musicians which piece to take from their folders to perform. Imagine the chaos if musicians were left individually to choose which pieces they were to play.

Those who work with youth and the youth themselves must also share an approach to ministry. The youth ministry coordinator guides those involved to choose and implement a perspective on youth ministry that will guide all that is done. The following paragraphs describe an approach to ministry that a growing number of churches and youth ministry coordinators are adopting.

Youth ministry is all a church does with and for youth, workers with youth, and parents of youth.—All of youth ministry is designed to bring young people to God through Christ and to develop them as believers. Ministry that includes parents and workers as well as youth is the most effective way to reach this goal.

Parents have a significant influence on their teenagers. This is true even during a period of life when young people are establishing some sense of separate identity from their parents. Parents and their teenage children still share a powerful, emotional bond; and they still spend many hours together.

Unfortunately, parents have the same power to influence negatively as positively. Church leaders who hope to see permanent, positive growth in the lives of youth must care about the influence of the home. Youth ministry that makes a lasting difference must include ministry with the parents of youth.

Youth ministry is also a ministry to and with other youth workers. The needs of youth in the 1990s are too great for one person. When a youth ministry coordinator counsels, motivates, inspires, encourages, or trains a youth worker, he or she is benefiting the teenagers. The youth ministry coordinator is multiplying his or her influence by directing it through other adults who also care for youth.

In some churches the youth ministry coordinator may be the only adult who works with youth. That leader is certainly a key person making a valuable contribution. Were it not for leaders in churches such as these, the spiritual outlook for their youth would be less promising.

Almost all youth ministry coordinators, including those in large churches, continually experience the shortage of other leaders. Even though it is a challenge, gently and consistently looking for others to share the load is a vital part of youth ministry.

Youth ministry is a shared ministry.—In a previous era of youth ministry, churches spoke of *giving* their youth a youth program. Today the emphasis is more on ministry *with* youth than on ministry *to* youth.

Teenagers are not fully developed adults, but they are not children either. They demonstrate their growing maturity in many arenas. Teenagers with jobs are often responsible for hundreds or thousands of dollars of equipment or inventory. Youth at school lead student organizations, organize extracurricular events, and do outstanding work in competitions. With training and encouragement those same youth can take leadership at church.

In small churches all youth can experience the advantage of active involvement in planning and implementing the youth program. They can enjoy roles that in large churches are often reserved for just a small percentage of youth group members.

Youth ministry is centered around the youth program organi-

zations.—A decade or two ago most churches viewed youth activities as "the youth program." Leaders in churches which had no specific youth activities would often report, "We have no youth program."

As has been noted earlier, the youth program is all that a church is doing with and for teenagers. That means that the classes and groups youth attend at church are part of the youth program. Youth Sunday School, youth music activities, Youth Discipleship Training, Acteens, Pioneer Royal Ambassadors, and High School Baptist Young Men are not only part of the youth program, they are the center of that program. Making these organizations more effective in evangelism, outreach, and teaching is a top priority.

Ideally, each church should provide for youth each of the groups listed above. That ensures that every area of Christian growth and discipleship will be addressed. Realistically, many smaller churches are missing one or more organizations.

The youth ministry coordinator should gently and consistently move toward providing each organization. In some churches the youth ministry coordinator may need to work for several years to achieve this worthy goal.

Youth activities have a vital role in youth ministry. They provide a way to reach many significant goals such as supporting outreach, building peer relationships, and providing a healthy use of leisuretime. The best activities support and complement the work of the ongoing youth organizations.

What the Youth Ministry Coordinator Does
No job description for the youth ministry coordinator would apply everywhere. Each church has a unique set of expectations, history, and resources that will shape the position. Here are several duties that would be common to many churches.

Lead the youth program to be evangelistic.—A youth ministry doesn't become evangelistic automatically. It becomes evangelistic because members intentionally plan and pray for it to be. The youth ministry coordinator should take a lead in shaping a youth ministry that introduces teenagers to Christ.

Support the work of the youth organizations.—Youth ministry coordinators who consider the youth organizations as vital to the youth program will want to do all they can to support those organizations. Specific ideas for giving that support are presented in chapter 3 of this book.

Work with the church nominating committee in enlisting adults to work with youth.—Most nominating committees welcome help as they search for adults who unconditionally love teenagers and are willing to help lead them.

Ensure that the youth workers get the training they need.—Some youth ministry coordinators feel comfortable providing training themselves. Others help workers take advantage of existing training opportunities.

Guide the Youth Ministry Council.—Ideally, a Youth Ministry Council is composed of several representative youth, several representative youth workers, and a youth parent or two. In very small churches, all the youth, workers, and parents can form the council.

The Youth Ministry Council considers needs and then plans a youth program that can meet those needs. The youth ministry coordinator is in the best position to coordinate and guide the work of the council. (For more information about organizing and working with a council, see *The Youth Ministry Council Guidebook* by Richard Ross, available by calling 1-800-458-BSSB, or from Baptist Book Stores.)

Coordinate the youth program calendar with the churchwide calendar.—The Youth Ministry Council takes the lead in creating the youth program calendar. The youth ministry coordinator takes the lead in coordinating that calendar with the churchwide calendar.

The youth program calendar should be supportive of such events as a churchwide revival, Sunday School Preparation Week, Vacation Bible School, January Bible Study, Baptist Doctrine Study, Christian Home Emphasis, and foreign and home missions studies. Also, the youth program calendar should support special events planned by the church staff or Church Council, such as a high attendance Sunday or a churchwide picnic.

If the church has a Church Council, the youth ministry coordinator should meet with the council to coordinate calendars. If the church has no council, the coordinator should communicate with the church staff about pending youth ministry plans. (For specific help in creating a balanced, comprehensive youth ministry calendar, see *Youth Ministry Planbook 4*, compiled by Richard Ross, available by calling 1-800-458-BSSB, or from

Baptist Book Stores.)

Plan and administer the youth ministry budget.—Most small churches now adopt annual budgets. Youth ministry should be an identifiable item in those budgets. Some churches have failed to budget for youth ministry simply because no one took the initiative to lead out in this area. A committed youth ministry coordinator may be able to lead the church to strengthen financial support for the youth program. (For specific help in planning a youth ministry budget, see chapter 8 in this book and *Youth Ministry Planbook 4.*)

Coordinate promotion of the youth program.—The youth ministry coordinator should work with Youth Ministry Council members to develop publicity and promotion. The coordinator may accept responsibility for publications such as the church bulletin or newsletter.

Printing and distributing the youth calendar is excellent promotion. In smaller youth groups calling every youth before special events may be a possibility.

Lead youth to Christ.—Leaders in smaller churches are better able to know the spiritual condition of almost every youth. This allows leaders and even mature youth to pray and plan for the salvation of specific teenagers.

With forethought, almost every youth activity or emphasis can help guide youth toward a personal commitment of faith. The youth ministry coordinator should keep this goal before the Youth Ministry Council as they plan.

The youth ministry coordinator should also take the lead in personally sharing with lost teenagers. Coordinators who develop a life-style of witnessing create a climate that encourages other youth and adults to begin to share.

Provide help for troubled youth.—These are not easy days to be a teenager. Factors such as divorce of parents, pressure from peers, and the negative influence of media have multiplied the number and intensity of crises affecting youth. Even small youth groups often have one or more youth struggling with issues such as chemical addiction, sexual misbehavior, abuse, or suicidal tendencies.

The youth ministry coordinator should take the lead in finding help for troubled youth. The coordinator can provide essential, personal support and spiritual counsel. In addition, the coordinator may feel the need to refer teenagers to competent,

Christian professionals in the community. Those referrals are best made when the coordinator has done research on the professionals available before the actual need arises. (For a thorough study on crises facing youth today, see *Ministry with Youth in Crisis*, compiled by Richard Ross and Judi Hayes. For help in responding to youth already in a crisis, see the audiotape series, *The 24-Hour Counselor: Youth Crisis Edition*, Volumes 1 and 2, compiled by Richard Ross. These are available by calling 1-800-458-BSSB, or from Baptist Book Stores.)

Coordinate ministry with the parents of youth.—The youth ministry coordinator should guide the Youth Ministry Council to include specific plans for parents of teenagers. As noted earlier, ministry to and with parents is a vital part of youth ministry.

Parents from two or more families might respond well to a monthly support group meeting. Other possibilities include parent and youth fellowships, retreats, dialogues, and missions projects.

Parents from several smaller churches might enjoy combining for a special seminar that would feature a community doctor, counselor, or school official. The associational youth ministry coordinator (or associational youth director) could take the lead in planning such an event. (For specific help in planning events that involve parents, see *Ministry with Youth and Their Parents*, by Richard Ross and Wade Rowatt, Jr., available by calling 1-800-458-BSSB, or from Baptist Book Stores.)

The youth ministry coordinator is a valuable person. With this committed leader as conductor, youth ministry can be balanced, exciting, and effective.

Personal Learning Activities

1. How is a youth ministry coordinator like a symphony conductor?

2. Why is a youth ministry coordinator needed?

3. What are the tasks of the youth ministry coordinator?

Chapter Three

Creating Effective Youth Organizations

YOUTH SUNDAY SCHOOL
Myrte Veach

Myrte Veach is senior manager of the Youth Program Section, Sunday School Youth-Adult Department, Sunday School Board, Nashville, Tennessee.

I grew up in a small town and a small Southern Baptist church in South Texas. I received loving care and attention from my immediate family and from my church family. They knew me and cared about me. They loved me and were concerned about what was important to me.

I was involved in every facet of church life. I learned about responsibility and commitment. I learned about weeping for lost people. I learned about ministry and caring. I learned about dedication and service.

One of my most pleasant memories is making a pledge as a child to help build a new church building. I was proud as I returned home during my freshman year in college for the note burning on that new church building—my church building that I had helped plan and pay for. What a glorious experience, growing up in a small church! I thank God for that!

An important part of any youth ministry is its Sunday School. In fact, an effective Youth Sunday School is essential to youth ministry in the small church.

I believe that Sunday School on Sunday morning ought to be the most exciting and demanding time in the life of a youth. Facing God's Word personally and directly should be a thrilling and challenging experience. I want youth to leave on Sunday morning knowing that they have stretched their minds and hearts in discovering God's Word. I want that study to captivate their minds and hearts so that they will go away from that church building aware of, believing in, and acting out of a basic youthism: Every teen needs to know Christ personally. That is the beginning, middle, and ending reason for having Youth Sunday School. Every youth in your community, every youth in your town, every youth in your state, every youth in this nation, every youth in this hemisphere, every youth in this world needs to know Christ!

The stated purpose for Sunday School is to reach people (youth) for Christ and church membership and through life-changing Bible study to lead them to grow through worshiping, witnessing, and ministering. An effective Youth Sunday School experience provides youth with the opportunity to accept Christ as personal Savior. It moves them to provide help in knowing how to share Christ with lost friends. It provides consistent opportunity for spiritual growth. It involves youth in learning how to help friends in need. It helps youth to reach beyond themselves to others in need in the community and around the world.

What Is an Effective Youth Sunday School?
Youth Sunday School is not something detached from you that you activate. You can't press a button and have it pop out. You can't start the computer and see it appear on the screen. You

can't turn the switch and fire it up. Youth Sunday School is something you create. Like a sculpture that comes alive, you take all the resources at hand (curriculum, workers, teens, and space), mesh them together, and pray that God's Spirit will make an effective Youth Sunday School. An effective Youth Sunday School requires you to touch it, massage it, and mold it; laugh and cry with it; be involved with it. A zap from afar or a wish that it would be better will not make it happen.

Youth Sunday School is a dynamic experience based in the Bible, centered on persons, and focused on life.

What Are the Guidelines for an Effective Youth Sunday School?

Keep the tasks or purposes of the Sunday School in your thinking as you plan Youth Sunday School.—These tasks are provided to keep you aware of the balance needed in an effective Youth Sunday School whatever its size. The tasks set forth the purposes of the Sunday School—the reasons we do Youth Sunday School. They are: (1) reaching youth for Bible Study, (2) teaching youth the Bible, (3) witnessing to youth about Christ and leading them into church membership, (4) ministering to Youth Sunday School members and nonmembers, (5) leading youth to worship, (6) interpreting to youth the work of the church and the denomination.

Organize the Youth Sunday School to meet youth needs.—The class is the basic unit in Youth Sunday School. Consider adding a second class when six to eight youth are enrolled. One class could be for older youth and one for younger youth, each with its own teacher. You already know how difficult providing for the needs and interests of a wide age span of youth in one group can be. If you have enough youth and workers to have two classes, then you might consider organizing into a department with a director and a teacher for each class.

Provide a dynamic Sunday morning experience.—Youth will continue to come to an experience that provides meaningful Bible study. All Youth Sunday School curriculum is developed around the concept of Total Period Teaching and provides helpful suggestions for your Sunday morning Bible study. Remember the youthism: I will never tell a teen anything I can lead him to discover for himself! You've heard that before, haven't you? That principle imparts all the following concepts. Follow your teacher's book as you look for these important elements for teaching youth:

• *Total Period Teaching.*—In this teaching concept the entire session relates to the "Central Bible Truth" of the Scripture passage and moves toward accomplishing the "Teaching Aim."

The "Central Bible Truth" is a one-sentence statement that reflects the heart of the Bible passage in terms of life today. The "Central Bible Truth" serves as the foundation of the Bible study experience. It is stated in present tense, active voice, concise words, and contemporary terms that are understandable and applicable to youth.

The "Teaching Aim" is the goal to which the teacher hopes to lead youth by the end of a session. Evangelistic opportunities for youth are provided in each session. Every teen needs to know Christ first, last, and forever!

• *Educational essentials.*—Motivation, examination, and application are the necessary educational components of the session. Workers will clearly identify these three educational essentials necessary for a successful teaching-learning experience in the teacher's book as:

1. Motivate the youth to learn. Create an interest in the Scripture study by capturing the attention of the youth. Help them to consider the potential value of the session's Bible study for their lives.

2. Examine the Bible passage. Search the Scriptures to understand the meaning to the original audience and to discover the meaning, value, and relevance of Bible truth to the lives of youth today.

3. Apply the Bible truth to life. Take the meaning, value, and relevance of Bible truths as one's own and then respond accordingly.

• *Learner involvement.*—Remember the principle, I will never tell teens anything I can lead them to discover for themselves! Most youth learn best what they are led to discover for themselves. Youth are capable of meaningful participation in the teaching-learning experience. Youth learn when they assume responsibility for their own spiritual development, including studying the lesson, preparing assignments for a session, or helping to plan units and sessions of study. Youth learn best when they are involved in Bible study through the use of various teaching-learning methods. The overall goal for Youth Sunday School includes helping youth to grow in Christian maturity, to think for themselves by relating Bible content and Bible truths to their lives.

Develop a strategy for keeping in touch with youth outside of Sunday morning.—Try to be involved in their lives in a consistent, ongoing way. Personal contact with youth beyond Sunday morning will allow you to know their needs and concerns even before they are spoken. Planning reaching and ministering activities for and with youth is not difficult if you are aware of their daily areas of concern. The telephone is your best tool for staying in touch with busy youth. Youth will be most open to you and impressed with your personal concern for them if you take the time to visit in their homes. Remember them on special days with a note or card.

Model a consistent, witnessing life-style.—Find ways to share your personal testimony with each youth in your class. Make the Sunday morning time an evangelistic opportunity for those lost youth who are in your class. Locate lost youth in the community and seek to involve them in the class.

Involve youth in all phases and responsibilities of Youth Sunday School.—Youth Sunday School is done with youth and not to youth. Consider using one of the leaders of the youth as the youth class leader. Let this youth become a partner with you as the teacher, reacher, and minister of the class.

Find ways to plan for good things to happen in your Youth Sunday School.—Planning needs to take place even if you are the only worker with youth in your church. Involve youth in helping you plan. Involve parents in helping you plan. Certainly involve the Holy Spirit in your planning.

Consider earning a Sunday School Leadership Diploma.—Order a *Church Study Course Catalog* from your state Sunday School director's office. Review the courses available, and order the books suggested for the Youth Sunday School Leadership Diploma. These books will provide many suggestions for making your Youth Sunday School more effective.

Keep the church informed and involved in the activities of the Youth Sunday School.

Pray for the leadership of the Holy Spirit as you work with this vital and important age group.

Read BREAKTHROUGH: Youth Sunday School Work.

DISCIPLESHIP TRAINING
R. Clyde Hall, Jr.

R. Clyde Hall is manager of the Youth Section, Discipleship Training Department, Sunday School Board, Nashville, Tennessee.

Christian youth need opportunities to grow as disciples. The program of Discipleship Training has as its task equipping persons for discipleship and personal ministry. "Discipleship is the Christian's lifelong commitment to the person, teaching, and spirit of Jesus Christ. Life under Jesus' lordship involves progressive learning, growth in Christlikeness, application of biblical truth, responsibility for sharing the Christian faith, and responsible church membership."[1]

Discipleship Training is for all youth and should be provided by all churches. In the Sermon on the Mount, Jesus proclaimed ethical and doctrinal teachings to the five thousand who were gathered there. In addition, Jesus had a special relationship with the twelve whom he taught in a more intense way. In fact, the New Testament seems to indicate that he also spent more time with Peter, James, and John, and perhaps even more time with John than he did with others of the twelve. A youth discipleship ministry should be modeled after the New Testament example. Such a discipleship ministry with youth is called by many DiscipleLife. A youth leader has a responsibility to all youth (the five thousand) as well as to the small group (the twelve) or the one. Discipleship training should be provided for all groups of youth in at least three ways:

Weekly Discipleship Training

This type of discipleship training (usually on Sunday) should be based on perceived needs of youth. What do youth need to know about what the Bible teaches concerning doctrine, the work of a church, and how to live the Christian life? Here are some keys to success:

Sharing leadership.—Shared leadership means that youth and adults work together in planning and conducting learning sessions, special studies, and projects. Shared leadership in a group occurs when the youth are in the meeting area early each week getting things ready for the planned activities; when the youth are encouraging others to enlist members into the group; and when a youth is leading the learning activities, the discussion, and the prayer time.

Choosing the right approach.

1. Individual.—Discipleship training with youth can take various approaches. By placing a book in the hands of a youth who has a particular need dealt with in the book, an adult can facilitate individual study by youth. A wise leader will follow up later to see how the youth is doing and what questions have been raised or answers discovered.

2. One-to-one.—One-to-one training takes place when an adult guides youth through *Survival Kit for New Christians, Youth Edition* or counsels a new Christian using *Commitment Counseling Manual.* In one-to-one study the youth and adult or two youth meet once a week to reinforce their individual reading and study for any Youth Discipleship Training resource.

3. Small group.—In small group study, the functions of study, planning, and leading are shared by an adult and a youth. An adult and youth also share responsibilities for maintaining group spirit, sharing concerns of members, and building the group through outreach and fellowship.

Choosing the right curriculum.—Each Youth Discipleship Training periodical is biblically based, practical, and personal. Focal passages of Scripture are selected for each session and unit. The content, developed out of the focal passage, applies to the content areas of Discipleship Training: Christian discipleship and personal ministry, Christian theology and Baptist doctrine, Christian ethics, Christian history, and church polity and organization. Youth are encouraged to apply biblical concepts to their daily lives as they deal with day-by-day and week-by-

34

week actions to achieve growth. The material in the periodicals is designed to meet the needs of youth for discipleship development. Each unit of study in Discipleship Training youth periodicals (*Youth Alive, The Youth Disciple, Baptist Youth*) contains ideas for the youth enlistment leader and detailed suggestions for the youth study leader to use in planning weekly learning sessions. In *equipping youth* adults and youth will find additional helps for planning all the events and experiences of the Youth Discipleship Training program (Disciple-Life). Leaders' materials are *Youth Alive Leaders' Packet, The Youth Disciple Leaders' Packet*, and *Baptist Youth Kit for Leaders*.

Choosing the right organization plan.—Do not feel discouraged if your small group is very small. One adult and one youth can be a group and share exciting learning experiences. Great potential lies within each person. If your group has fewer than seven youth, one adult leader can handle both the study and enlistment functions. Consider the following organizational model:

Small-Group Organizational Model

DiscipleLife Training Group Leader (an adult) Youth Study Leader	DiscipleLife Training Group Enlistment Leader (an adult) Youth Enlistment Leader

Planning each session.

1. Unit-session planning.—The DiscipleLife training group leader meets with the youth study leader for each unit two weeks before the unit begins. Prior to the planning meeting, each should read the unit of study in the youth periodical and the leaders' guide. (*Baptist Youth* contains both youth and leader material.) Pull the items for the unit from the leaders' kit/packet.

The DiscipleLife training group leader and the study leader will each need one Unit Plan Sheet and a Session Plan Sheet for each session in the unit. You may duplicate the plan sheets provided in the kit/packet. Use the plan sheets to do the following.

• Consider the unit and session goals in the leader's guidance material. Write your goals for the unit and sessions based on the needs of group members.

• Decide how you will use the activities in the session guidance to accomplish the learning goals. List the agenda.

• List the materials and other resources you will need to gather to conduct the sessions. (See "Before the Session.")

• Write the names of other group members to whom you will make assignments.

• Decide how you will arrange the room each Sunday.

2. Enlistment planning.—The Enlistment Plan Sheet in the leaders' packet/kit will guide the training group enlistment leader and youth enlistment leader in planning ways to advertise the study and enroll new members. Enlistment ideas are included in *Youth Alive Leaders' Guide*, *The Youth Disciple Leaders' Guide*, and *Baptist Youth*. Enlistment planning includes the following.

• Promoting/advertising the training group study.

• Contacting prospects and involving them in the group.

• Informing the group regarding concerns of members and special happenings in their lives.

• Encouraging members' participation in DiscipleLife projects and special studies.

Weekday Discipleship Training
You cannot meet all of youth's needs for discipleship development through only one method. Various options are needed to capture youth's attention, challenge them, and equip them for dynamic Christian living. Weekday Discipleship Training provides options for learning and growing with experience-centered approaches.

Weekday Discipleship Training courses last for short time periods, with a definite beginning and ending (usually 3 to 13 sessions). Many books for these studies are developed for four or five one-hour sessions. They make excellent resources for camps, retreats, and weekday events.

Plan Discipleship Training courses to meet needs of the entire youth group throughout the year. Include them in your annual calendar of youth activities. As you plan a special summer mission trip, you can prepare the youth for the experience by requiring them to study certain resources.

36

Annual Youth Discipleship Projects

Provide annual experiential youth projects for youth such as Youth Week, Youth Bible Drill, Youth Speakers' Tournament, and DiscipleYouth. Schedule these projects at times other than the training group meeting time.

Weekly Discipleship Training (usually Sunday) and Weekday Discipleship Training are types of Discipleship Training for the 5,000. DiscipleYouth is Discipleship Training for the twelve. DiscipleYouth is an in-depth process for training youth in the discipline of discipleship and in equipping them with witnessing skills.

For further information in implementing Discipleship Training for youth see *DiscipleAll: A Discipleship Training Manual*, chapter 4.

Y O U T H   M U S I C
John Booth

John Booth is professor of church music, Hannibal LaGrange Collegeok, Hannibal, Missouri.

Unlike Sunday School and Discipleship Training, youth choir has no suggested curriculum or lesson plan. While many sources offer good literature, that choice is more at the discretion of the leader than other church programs. If you are in your 30s or 40s, you remember the era that produced early youth musicals. At that time they were the youth's bright ray of hope in a sea of adult music. We are fortunate now to have music written for both the ear of youth and to help train and develop the youth's voice.

Sunday to Sunday

What we do week-to-week in youth choir is probably more important than the extensive, more visible projects. Two elements must be considered—rehearsal and performance. A good rehearsal has some important elements.

Planned to the minute.—Start on time, stop on time, and have everything you do written out. If you are working with an uncertain accompanist, a written schedule will give provide security by showing what is ahead.

Controlled.—This is less of a problem if the rehearsal is planned. Go one-on-one outside rehearsal for serious discipline problems.

A mix of Christian top 40 and material that can develop and train the voice.—Youth musicals can be positive experiences; but if your diet is only musicals, you are taking the easy way out and may be shortchanging their voices.

If you are starting in a small church, allow yourself time to reach your goal. If your goal is to have youth lead worship rather than be performers, you may need to bring them along slowly. Youth need to know that we want them to have choir experiences so that they can help lead in worship. Many youth in our culture are seeking structure and discipline. Becoming a worship leader can be affirming in that they see the support of the entire congregation. Most churches that have never had a youth choir are thrilled to see youth participate in worship. The youth may sing once a quarter or once a month, but they may eventually sing every week. To do that they will have to build a repertoire from which they can draw favorites. After a year you could list everything they've sung and have them vote for 10 favorites. That immediately becomes either a "Favorites Youth Choir Reunion" or 10 for the next year.

A serious word of warning—if you are reaching unchurched youth, your choir music may be their first theology lesson. The things you pick must reflect the essence of the gospel.

Choir Tours

These words strike both fear and joy in the hearts of leaders. We all have a mental photo album, and the words *choir tour* could call up different images. Many of us shy away from trying to take our choir on tour because we are comparing ourselves to the big churches. God has a ministry for both large and small churches. We are to serve at our own church in the spirit that God put us here and we would rather be here than anywhere else.

We can learn from every church, large and small. If you have never toured, offer to go as an extra adult with a church that

38

tours regularly. Learn from the success of others and be glad for what God is doing with them.

Music Only?

We have gone through periods of time when choirs have almost felt guilty if they did a music-only tour. If all we do is sing, then the guilt may be real. However, if we are salt and light as we go, our song takes on new meaning and impact. We must have something to say and we must go out with the underlying motive to spread the gospel. We must also trust the Spirit of God to take the truth sung and use it to convict.

Teaching and Ministry

You might want to get in a youth leaders' meeting at the associational or state level and poll other leaders about music and other projects. Listed below are a few to start your thinking.

Backyard Bible Clubs.—Conducting Backyard Bible Clubs can bring you into closer contact with the people to whom you will sing in evening concerts. Children and parents can be invited to evening activities. Attending Backyard Bible Clubs may encourage persons to enroll in regular Bible study.

"Tough It" Tour.—If you are large enough to tour, some churches smaller than yours cannot afford to feed and house your choir. Some or all of a tour can be done by cooking your own meals and sleeping in churches. Though it can be hard on leaders, it can build community among your youth. If you use live instruments, you can have a jam session with youth from both the host and the visiting church staying up late and singing together.

Ministry project.—The Home Mission Board needs small groups of youth to do a variety of ministry projects. Any church could look into the possibility of ministering in resort missions or in the inner city.

If you are one of those rare youth choirs in a mission area, part of your ministry may be that of giving challenge, hope, and encouragement to churches who have yet to discover their musical potential. They watch you present your musical and realize that they could do the same. The most rewarding part of a choir tour is when that church calls you the next year to borrow your music so they can go out to sing and minister. Planting new choirs is almost like planting new churches.

Ensembles

No matter how small the group, if it is the only youth musical group, call it a choir. If you have an ensemble, let participation in the ensemble be in addition to youth choir.

Vocal Groups

Two possibilities are to select a group or to include whoever wants to participate. If you select the group, here are some guidelines to follow:

If you hold auditions, use some help from outside the church.—If you have to choose between two, you want another set of ears.

Balance between music ability and relationship skills.—If your ensembles are outreach groups, you will need youth who can minister to needs and share their faith.

Require youth who sing ensembles to be faithful to other ministries of the church.—They are earning the right to participate.

Find a place for the uncertain singer but enthusiastic youth to travel with the group.—This person can operate the sound system or other technical equipment. The enthusiasm will be contagious.

Reaudition every year.

Consider having a nonaudition group for younger voices.—This training will improve the quality of the ensemble in the future.

Instrumental Groups

Parents in your church have already funded the cost of your instrumental ensemble. If you are not a trained musician, you can learn some simple rules to help you put music in the right key for the right instruments. If you are totally in the dark, ask a musician in your church for help. Many youth know how to transpose for their own instruments.

Handbells

Though the initial cost is high, the long-term benefits in music education and beauty in worship are worth the cost. Youth are the focus in this book, but all ages can learn to play handbells. Often a memorial gift or one-time offering is a great way to fund the cost of handbells and pay cash for them.

40

Seasonal Programs
Even if you do not have a youth choir, you still have a youth music program. Seasonal emphases (Christmas, Easter, local celebrations, mission studies) provide a chance for pilot involvement with youth. Those youth who are not comfortable singing may be able to do drama, sound, lighting, ushering, promotion, or other details. Be careful, however, that teens are not branded as singers and nonsingers. Some youth may find their voice if exposed to choir experiences. You should also not brand youth as soprano, alto, tenor, or bass.

Many youth begin their choir experiences in adult choir and often for Easter or Christmas cantatas. While this is not ideal, it at least is a way to involve them. Some youth in small churches have dual membership in youth and adult choirs. College and career young adults may enjoy singing with the youth for special programs. They can be used as player-coaches in youth choir.

Many association and state groups offer music experiences for youth. Those who have no youth choir can go to these. Youth may catch the excitement and take it home.

At the associational level churches can band together for a summer presentation of a musical and maybe perform it round-robin in each church or in a central location. Music leaders can divide up duties and act as accompanists, sound or lighting people. At rehearsal they can teach voice parts to different sections.

Churches without choirs need to be aware of community or parachurch groups. These organizations tend to become self-supporting and independent, diluting youth's loyalty to church. The best guidelines for parachurch involvement are:

1. Leaders hold the local church in high esteem.
2. Youth get permission from pastor and/or youth minister to be involved.
3. Local church gets first place. Parachurch groups plan around the church's schedule.
4. Projects are terminal rather than continuing.

A C T E E N S
Marti Solomon

Marti Solomon is Acteens consultant, Woman's Missionary Union, Birmingham, Alabama.

Youth need to understand God's mandate to "Go into all the world." You need to provide quality missions education for your youth. Acteens will do that for the girls in your church. You can have a successful Acteens organization, no matter what the size. In fact, many of the most active Acteens organizations come from small churches.

You can start Acteens with only one teenage girl and one adult leader. Of course, that leader is important. Look for someone who loves youth and is willing to invest the time to make the organization work.

The Acteens leader will need some materials to get started. The *Acteens Leader Manual* will tell her about the organization and her role in it. She will need *Accent Leader Edition* for herself and *Accent* for the girls involved. *Accent* is the magazine for Acteens which contains the study curriculum as well as suggested activities and other missions information and is available through the Woman's Missionary Union, (205) 991-8100.

The Acteens organization is unique because it involves girls in the mission task of the church. Acteens study and put into action the things they have learned. Through Acteens, girls are led to make missions an important part of their lives. Girls also develop skills in leadership and planning in Acteens. A strong Acteens organization is built on prayer and encourages girls to go the extra mile in seeking out and responding to needs around them.

As a Woman's Missionary Union organization, Acteens share in the four tasks performed by WMU in the church:
- Teach missions.

- Engage in mission action and personal witnessing.
- Support missions.
- Interpret and undergird the work of the church and the denomination.

Since the fourth task is one that is shared with all the church programs, let's look at the first three, which are unique to Acteens, and consider how they can easily be carried out in a small organization.

Teach Missions

In teaching missions, Acteens leads girls to a growing understanding of God's missionary purpose and encourages response to that purpose in commitment and obedience. Mission study for Acteens includes the biblical basis of missions, progress of Christian missions, contemporary missions, and the spiritual development of the Acteens.

An Acteens organization meets weekly for study. The units of study in *Accent* are designed for organizations of all sizes. Following directions given, the leader can easily adapt some of the learning procedures for a small group.

In addition to the units of study found in *Accent*, Acteens have opportunities to be involved in other study projects. At times, these are coed projects in which the Pioneer Royal Ambassadors and High School Baptist Young Men participate with the Acteens. Acteens may involve all of the youth in the youth group in some study projects.

The most familiar of these all-youth study projects are the annual home missions study and foreign missions study. The home missions study, conducted in February, prepares for participation in the March observance of the Week of Prayer for Home Missions. The foreign missions study in November prepares for participation in the Week of Prayer for Foreign Missions in December.

Acteens are also encouraged to become involved in individual mission study. This includes studying *Accent* and other missions materials, books, and videotapes.

Engage in Mission Action and Personal Witnessing

These two parts of the same task, mission action and personal witnessing, are different in definition but similar in purpose. Mission action is ministering and witnessing to persons of special need or circumstance who are not members of the church or its programs; mission action is also combating social and moral problems. Personal witnessing is a Christian's sharing the gospel of Jesus Christ with another person and giving that person an opportunity to confess Jesus Christ as Savior and Lord. These two go together because personal witnessing should be the natural follow-through to mission action.

Through Acteens, girls have opportunities to reach out beyond the walls of the church and become aware of and respond to the needs of their world. They experience the satisfaction of knowing they have brought some happiness into someone's life. Through working to combat social and moral problems, they have the sense of improving their community.

Mission action and personal witnessing can be done effectively with a small group. In many cases a large group would be intimidating to those who are the objects of their ministry and witness.

People with special needs or circumstances to whom Acteens can minister and witness include prisoners, military personnel, alcoholics, drug abusers, the poor, unchurched groups, language groups, internationals, migrants, travelers and tourists, nonreaders, senior adults, unwed parents, juvenile delinquents, the sick, handicapped, latchkey children, the institutionalized, the abused, and minority groups. Target issues include social and moral problems which victimize people such as family problems, gambling, pornography, obscenity, alcoholism, drug abuse, race relations, and economic and political problems. These long lists are good indications that one doesn't have to look far to find someone in need of ministry and witness.

Support Missions
Acteens support missions in five ways:

1. Praying for missions invovles communicating with God on behalf of missionaries and missions work.

2. Giving to missions involves providing financial support of missions work being conducted for churches through the Cooperative Program, the Annie Armstrong Easter Offering for Home Missions, the Lottie Moon Christmas Offering for Foreign Missions, and state missions offerings.

3. Providing personal ministries for missionaries and their

families includes providing words of encouragement and acts of kindness such as writing letters, calling, caring for children and parents, making transportation and housing available, and providing other needed ministries.

4. Emphasizing the need for persons to become involved in mission service includes helping to create and sustain an environment in which Acteens can hear and respond to God's call to mission service. Nurturing the persons who repsond to God's call to mission service includes providing support, information, and encouragement to help Acteens follow God's leadership into mission service.

5. Being involved in volunteer mission service involves participating in missions projects in support of missions work being conducted by representative programs and agencies.

Much of mission support is individual in nature. As a result, the size of your group has no bearing on it. It only takes one girl to pray, to give, to write a missionary, to respond to God's call, to make a difference. Being involved in volunteer mission service can be done individually or as a group. Many think that to do a mission trip you must have many youth. On the contrary, small groups can minister in areas that could not accommodate a large group. A program for older Acteens called Acteens Activators involves girls in just this type of mission trip. If you prefer for all of your youth to be involved, the Acteens can serve as a core group on which to build, and the Acteens leader can be an excellent resource person.

Studiact
Studiact is the individual achievement plan for Acteens. It gives Acteens opportunities to work independently toward meeting goals they set for themselves. They work alone on activities which are based on the above tasks. Studiact is done effectively in a small group because the Acteen is not dependent on others to get the work done.

Acteens is an exciting way to provide quality missions education for your small youth group.

PIONEER ROYAL AMBASSADORS AND HIGH SCHOOL BAPTIST YOUNG MEN
Mike Day

Mike Day is editor, High School Baptist Young Men's materials, Brotherhood Commission, Memphis, Tennessee.

Missions education is important to any youth ministry—large or small. If the goal of your youth ministry is to develop spiritually mature and well-balanced young people, missions education is a must. Missions education organizations provide something for young people that no other church program organization provides—awareness of and involvement in missions and ministry.

Missions Education for Male Teenagers
The Pioneer Royal Ambassador and High School Baptist Young Men organizations work together to provide quality missions education and missions involvement experiences for males in grades 7-12. Pioneers (for grades 7-9) and HSBYM (for grades 10-12) involve boys and young men in missions activities, teach historical and contemporary missions effectively, lead youth to support missions through prayer and giving, help young males develop a personal sense of ministry, and make youth aware of how Southern Baptists work together to accomplish our missions task. Both programs use a variety of methods to accomplish the tasks mentioned above.

Regular meetings.—Regular chapter and unit meetings provide quality missions education in a learning laboratory setting for males in grades 7-12.

Pioneer Royal Ambassadors are organized into chapters that meet on a set day, at a set time, each week for missions study.

Curriculum material for these weekly study meetings is published in *RA Leadership*, a quarterly publication of the Brotherhood Commission.

High School Baptist Young Men meet at least once a month for missions study and hold additional meetings, at the discretion of the HSBYM unit, for missions and interest involvement. The HSBYM program is intentionally less structured than the Pioneer RA program to accommodate the needs, schedule, and life-style of older youth.

Advancement/personal development.—In addition to regular meetings, Pioneer RAs and High School Baptist Young Men provide opportunities for young men to study about and be involved in missions at their own pace and as a result of their own motivation. This self-study program is called advancement for Pioneers and personal development for High School Baptist Young Men.

Boys in grades seven through nine have the opportunity to progress through the Pioneer Adventure program and discover their gifts for missions involvement. The four-level program is progressive with each level leading to deeper commitment. Pioneer RAs are recognized and rewarded for completion of each level of the program.

Through Missions Challenge young men in grades 10-12 are encouraged to invest up to 750 hours in missions study and missions involvement. Young men are recognized for their accomplishments at various points along the journey, and scholarships from Baptist colleges and universities are available for those who complete the entire program.

Missions activities.—Through involvement in missions activities, Pioneer RAs and High School Baptist Young Men grow in their commitment to missions and mature in their Christian experience. Missions activities are designed to meet a specific need for a specific target group by a specific action.

Meaningful relationships.—Both programs of missions education for males in grades 7-12 place major emphasis on the development of meaningful relationships. The organizations strengthen relationships between teenagers and Christ, their church, their families, other adults, and their peers. The strengthening of these relationships opens the door to greater spiritual maturity.

Interest activities.—Using interest-oriented activities in Pioneer Royal Ambassador and High School Baptist Young Men can provide teaching avenues and learning experiences and can enhance the total program. Such activities may include camping, games, sports, hobbies, and some coed activities.

Pioneer RAs and HSBYM in the Small Church
Both programs of missions education for youth have the goal of involving boys and young men in missions. Both use a variety of approaches to accomplish this goal. And both can be easily implemented in a small church.

The full-scale approach.—Many churches, though small, are able to implement full-scale Pioneer Royal Ambassador and High School Baptist Young Men's organizations. Though total church membership is limited, the church may have enough young men in grades 7-12 to organize chapters and units. Such organization requires sufficient membership and leadership. The counselor for Pioneer RAs and the advisor for HSBYM may be the same person if the situation dictates it.

The point here is simple—church size does not necessarily dictate the size of a missions education group. The number of junior-high and high-school students in the church and community and a church's vision are determining factors.

Monthly meetings.—High School Baptist Young Men and Pioneer Royal Ambassadors are designed to be more than just one-meeting-a-month programs. However, a lack of adult leadership, a crowded weekly church program schedule, a crowded high-school and work schedule of members, or the lack of some other important resources may cause a church to consider having monthly missions education meetings. This would involve a unit meeting at a set time and place once a month for the purpose of mission study. An obvious disadvantage would be the young men's lack of exposure to other phases of the programs such as personal development, missions activities, and interest activities. Another option is to adapt all four aspects of the programs into the meetings. Such adaptation carries limitations of not being complete in any one area. Another option is to use a different aspect (i.e., advancement/personal development) of the programs as the focus of each meeting.

One-to-one.—If a church believes that missions education is not for them because the church has only one young man in their church to take advantage of the program, this alternate approach will work. This approach involves one young man and one adult serving as his counselor or adviser.

What can just one man and one young man accomplish? The possibilities are unlimited. Two people can engage in meaningful missions study using meeting plans found in *RA Leadership* and *High School Baptist Young Men's Planbook*.

One young man can have an impressive impact on his small corner of the world by giving up to 750 hours of volunteer Christian service to his community through involvement in *Missions Challenge*, the personal development phase of HSBYM. Two people can do a lot of praying for global missions. Two people can participate in many games, sports, crafts, and outdoor adventures as partners. A meaningful Christian relationship can be formed between a man and a young man developing a one-to-one High School Baptist Young Men's program.

Associational units.—Associations composed primarily of small churches may begin one Pioneer RA chapter or HSBYM unit for the entire association. A team of advisers may be enlisted from several churches and officers elected from all available young men. The churches involved could share the expenses of the organization and provide the needed materials and literature. If enough young men are interested, more than one associational unit may be formed. This approach often works well in rural associations.

Community groups.—Small, inner-city churches may want to try a variation of the associational unit approach. The formation of a community RA chapter or HSBYM unit gives young men an opportunity to participate in a quality program. The unit may meet at the church or in a nearby home or other suitable location. Since High School Baptist Young Men encourages youth to lead themselves, this organization can fit any size church where high school students are found.

---

[1]From *Church Base Design 1986 Update*, II:51 © Copyright 1986 The Baptist Sunday School Board of the Southern Baptist Convention. All rights reserved.

Personal Learning Activities

1. What is the purpose of Sunday School? What steps can leaders take to make Sunday School special for youth in a small church?

2. What is the purpose of Discipleship Training? What kinds

of discipleship experiences do youth need to have?

3. Is singing the only purpose of youth choir? What kinds of musical experiences should a small church consider?

4. What are the three primary tasks of Acteens and how can they be accomplished in a small church?

5. What different possibilities exist for organizations for young men in missions education?

Chapter Four

Finding and Training Others to Share the Load

Judi S. Hayes

Judi S. Hayes is a design editor, Church Administration Department, Sunday School Board, Nashville, Tennessee.

You dream of all the wonderful programs discussed in the last chapter and of the exciting activities your youth would enjoy, but you just do not have the time to develop and lead them. Don't despair. Perhaps help is available. You may need to share your dreams for the youth and ask for help in not-so-obvious places.

Many adults, from college age to retirement, care about the youth in your church. Because your group is small, most of the adults know the youth. They have watched them grow, and they care about them. Like you, they probably want the church to provide the best for these teenagers.

But someone needs to organize the work, decide what leadership positions need to be filled, ask persons to accept various responsibilities, and equip the leaders for their tasks. As youth ministry coordinator, you probably are best suited for that job. Others in the church will help you—the nominating committee, for example—but someone must take the lead.

At first, you may feel overwhelmed. But a little planning and organization will help you to see just what is needed.

How Much Help Is Needed?

Begin by outlining the church's current youth ministry. A good place to start is with the program organizations mentioned in the last chapter. How many of those does your church currently have? Who works in those organizations now? Which areas are vacant and need to be filled right away? Which are in organizations you would like to start?

The next step may be to survey your congregation. Develop a form asking for their interest in the positions you need. But don't stop there. The adults you survey may have many talents useful to a youth ministry that may not appear on a list of program organization positions. Brainstorm with your Youth Ministry Council and nominating committee to list the positions needed and to ask adults to help your youth in other ways.

You can add many items to the list that are relevant for your church. You may have needs for persons with special equipment such as computers, VCRs, video cameras, etc. You also may want to add an open-ended item for adults to suggest contributions they can make that you have not listed. If your program organizations have many vacancies, you may want to survey the adults twice—once for ongoing leadership positions in program organizations and again later for other help.

Before giving the adults the survey to complete, find a time to talk with them about your dreams for youth ministry. Instead of just including a sheet in the weekly worship bulletin, plan a special time to ask the adults for help. The Youth Ministry Council may want to sponsor an after-church fellowship on Sunday night for all adults, or you may ask adult Sunday School directors if you can have a few minutes on Sunday morning to talk about the church's youth ministry and your dreams for the youth in your church. Be specific about the help

Youth Ministry Survey

Youth in our church need adults to work with them. Please check as many of the following as you would consider doing if asked. Be assured that this survey will not assume a commitment without personal conversations with you about all that is involved with each responsibility. Also, with each position comes the training needed to complete the task.

____ Direct one of these youth programs. (List those needed.)
____ Teach in one of these program areas. (List those needed.)
____ Serve as a substitute teacher.
____ Attend youth events as a sponsor.
____ Provide transportation for local youth events.
____ Accompany youth on overnight activities.
____ Drive a bus or van for out-of-town activities.
____ Take youth visiting.
____ Plan recreational activities for youth.
____ Provide refreshments for youth events.
____ Invite youth into your home.
____ Provide financial support for youth who cannot afford to attend some youth activities.
____ Counsel youth in crisis.
____ Lead parenting conferences in _____ . (Indicate area of interest.)
____ Coach a _____ team. (Indicate sport.)

you need and how adults can make the difference in what the church can do for and with its youth.

Who Can Help?

Everyone who can work well with youth may not respond to a survey. Some people may need a personal invitation; others may need a gentle nudge. And others may say, "Who, me?" They never have thought about working with youth.

Here are a few groups you'll want to include as you look for youth leaders:

Young adults.—Adults who are closest in age to youth can be real assets to the youth ministry. They have boundless energy to enjoy sports and other recreational activities with youth. They can stay up all night at a lockin on Friday and still have energy to go to work on Monday.

They are close enough in age to youth so that many youth will confide in them, relate well to them, and follow their examples. This demands that young adults who work with youth be mature and see themselves as leaders. But don't automatically eliminate a college-age young adult who may not always know where to draw the line between fun and folly. Just balance these adults with more mature leaders. Let college-age adults plan the recreational activities for an event, but plan to have older adults as sponsors. Then three age groups will benefit from your planning—youth, young adults, and middle-aged adults.

Senior adults.—Sometimes this group is overlooked as leaders for youth. Love of youth should be the determining factor rather than age. Many senior adults love youth and have time to spend with them. Senior adults may not want the ongoing responsibility of teaching a Sunday School class, but they will gladly take one or two youth on an outreach visit. They may not want to take the RAs camping, but many senior adults would enjoy taking that same group of young men on a fishing trip.

In an age when many youth seldom have the opportunity to spend much time with grandparents, the church can provide substitute relationships for youth and senior adults. Both groups will grow from the intergenerational contacts.

Parents of youth.—Parents of youth, who themselves are active church members, are already vitally interested in the church's youth ministry; and most are willing to work to provide an active, well-rounded ministry for their own youth. Some youth, however, who are struggling to begin the process of breaking away from parental control, do not want their parents working with them at church.

Sometimes parents can work in youth ministry but not in direct contact with their own youth. For example, a father of a teenage girl may teach a boys class in Sunday School. Or the mother of a teenage boy may work with an Acteens group. However, if separating youth from their parents is not possible, don't automatically dismiss them as possible youth workers. You may want to talk first with the youth involved and then with the parents to see how each feels about the parents' working with their own youth in some aspect of the church's youth ministry. Both parents and youth may feel comfortable with the parents' active involvement. And even youth who would rather not have a parent as a Sunday School teacher would be willing for Mom or Dad to sponsor youth events in their home or to accompany youth on some activities.

Where Can Youth Leaders Get the Training They Need?
Youth leaders need training in the program areas they lead and in understanding youth. Even experienced workers need refresher courses and the encouragement and motivation to build even better programs. Then ongoing training is needed in such areas as ministering to youth in crisis.

Training for new leaders.—Most state conventions and associations sponsor workshops each year for age-group leaders in all program organizations. Making this quality training available each year to all youth workers should motivate the youth ministry coordinator and the nominating committee to complete their work early enough for workers to plan to attend these meetings.

Because many churches come together for these meetings, leaders can share ideas, concerns, and questions with qualified trainers as well as workers from neighboring churches. The training sessions can become times of fellowship for youth leaders. Relationships may be built with other churches for future training and fellowship activities that would be difficult for a church to do alone. For example, several churches may decide to sponsor a career fair for high-school youth, or they may invite a doctor to talk about teen health concerns to parents of youth.

Youth leaders also may go to Ridgecrest or Glorieta for a week of training during the summer. Reservations are accepted beginning February 1 for summer conferences, and some weeks fill quickly. For information on the summer schedule, write or call Ridgecrest Baptist Conference Center, P. O. Box 128, Ridgecrest, NC 28770, (704) 669-8022; and Glorieta Baptist Conference Center, P. O. Box 8, Glorieta, NM 87535, (505) 757-6161.

Ongoing training.—Youth leaders can find ongoing training by meeting regularly for planning, training, and fellowship. For example, weekly workers meetings are a good planning time for Sunday School workers. These meetings take place on

Wednesdays in many churches.

Each program organization has Church Study Course books and administrative materials to train leaders. Study Course books can be studied individually or in groups. Credit is awarded for the completion of each, and diplomas are given when a series of books is completed. For a catalog describing diploma plans, write Church Study Course, Sunday School Board, 127 Ninth Avenue, North, Nashville, TN 37234. Your *Church Materials Catalog* and *Baptist Book Store Catalog* also have information about these resources.

Special training.—From time to time youth leaders may desire training in an area that requires a professional. Your church already may have a professional in the area needed. If not, you may want to communicate your church's need to your associational director of missions or to the associational youth ministry coordinator. If your youth leaders are feeling a need for training in some area, others in your area likely are experiencing that need.

If the association is unable to respond with training at this time, you may want to ask several churches in your area to join you in sponsoring a training event. Leaders for the event may be found in your community at local colleges or universities or at state or county institutions. For example, you may invite a youth guidance officer to talk about youth crime in your area. Or you may invite a medical doctor specializing in adolescent medicine to speak to a group about eating disorders. Some of these training events will benefit both parents and youth workers.

Any size church can have an active, comprehensive youth ministry with motivated, trained leaders. Take the time right now to make a chart showing all the youth leaders in all program organizations. Then begin to plan your next step for finding and training youth workers.

Personal Learning Activities
1. What preliminary steps should be taken before distributing a Youth Ministry Survey to adults in your church?

2. What needs in your youth ministry can be met by college-age young adults? by senior adults? by parents of youth?

3. How can your association help train youth workers? Whom should you call at your association office for help?

Chapter Five

Working with a Youth Ministry Council

Dennis M. Rogers

Dennis M. Rogers is associate director of the Church Training Department, Georgia Baptist Convention, Atlanta, Georgia.

According to recent Home Mission Board statistics almost a third of the approximately 37,500 churches in the Southern Baptist Convention have Sunday School enrollments of 150 or less. Youth enrollment in these churches is usually less than 30. This is significant when we are so prone to evaluate the success of a youth ministry on the basis of how many youth are participating. We often conclude that a numerically large church has a better youth program than a much smaller church because more youth are involved.

How do we adequately evaluate the effectiveness of ministry with youth in a local church? I don't believe we can find much evidence to support success based primarily on numerical size. Being part of a large youth group does have some advantages but also some disadvantages. Effectiveness has more to do with the long-term results of the programming and ministry with the youth, parents, and leaders than just the numbers of those participating.

One advantage youth have in small groups is the opportunity to have a leadership role. Youth in small churches can contribute much to the work of the church, and often they are seen more as a part of the total church rather than as one subgroup. The concept of a Youth Ministry Council not only takes youth seriously and involves them in meaningful leadership roles, but it also fosters results such as involvement, identity, and intimacy that make for a successful youth ministry in any size church.

The Youth Ministry Council in a Small Youth Group
Today the youth minister or youth ministry coordinator in a local church needs to reconsider the best way to involve significant others in youth ministry. For many years this involvement in many churches took the form of a youth council (made up of youth) and a youth committee (made up of adults). The youth council's purposes were to help the youth coordinator plan certain youth events and deal with any issue that the youth coordinator might bring before them. The youth committee's responsibilities were to assist the youth coordinator in determining what programming ideas suggested by the youth council were possible, to help in physical arrangements for programming, and to chaperone youth events.

Now youth ministry coordinators should consider another possibility for involving significant others (youth and adults) in youth ministry. This model of a Youth Ministry Council has representatives of three groups who work with the youth ministry coordinator—(1) designated youth who represent the entire youth group; (2) youth leaders who work with youth in Sunday School, Discipleship Training, Acteens, RAs and High School Baptist Young Men, and the youth music program; and (4) youth parents.

The Youth Ministry Council has several advantages over the old council/committee model. The youth ministry coordinator relates to only one planning group instead of two. The Youth

Ministry Council's adult members are all adults who are already directly involved in the youth ministry. Concerns of parents of youth are a priority.

A Youth Ministry Council has several benefits for a small youth group.

It provides an organizational plan for key adults working with youth in the youth program areas as well as representative youth and parents to meet together to plan and evaluate ministry goals and projects.—In churches where the number of youth and youth workers are relatively few, this model can be more easily implemented because of the limited number of people to include.

In a small church youth representation might be limited to three youth (one from grades 7 and 8, one from grades 9 and 10, and one from grades 11 and 12). The key adult from each youth organization also serves on the Council. That person may be a department director or perhaps the only adult who works in that organization. If an organization is not meeting at the present time (such as Youth Discipleship Training or a missions education organization), enlisting an adult who cares about youth to represent that area of need (discipleship, missions education, etc.) will strengthen the Council and provide balance in youth programming. If one of the adults is not a youth parent, one should be enlisted.

Guiding the Council is the youth ministry coordinator. One of the adults already mentioned may also serve as youth ministry coordinator. By naming a youth ministry coordinator, the church is indicating the person who has primary youth leadership responsibilities in the church whether he or she is a part-time employee of the church, a volunteer, or even a full-time employee (such as the pastor if he is functioning in that role).

The Youth Ministry Council model is intended to be flexible and adaptable, but it should represent youth, parents, and all youth organizations. One purpose of the Youth Ministry Council is to keep youth programming balanced.

It involves youth and adults along with the youth ministry coordinator in the planning and decision-making process.—A practical philosophy of a shared ministry means that youth and adults are able to offer insights and experiences in planning events and are able to bring unique gifts and talents into youth programming.

Implied in what has already been said is an understanding that young people can significantly contribute in the leadership role of the youth group. When youth are allowed and encouraged to assume meaningful leadership roles at church, they invariably become more confident in assuming leadership roles in other organizations.

It helps ensure youth involvement in church life.—Youth will support activities and programs they help plan. Youth genuinely feel they are being heard and are being given a responsible position alongside adults.

It can be a catalyst to help build a common bond of purpose.— In a small youth group the Youth Ministry Council can more easily assimilate the goals of individual youth into group objectives.

Because the Youth Ministry Council's adult membership is composed of key leaders from the youth organizations, those program organizations will be stronger.—Strong program organizations are the heart of an effect youth ministry.

This organizational plan for a Youth Ministry Council is based on the model of the Youth Ministry Council described in the *Youth Ministry Council Guidebook* by Richard Ross. It is an excellent resource for any size youth group.[1]

The Role of the Youth Ministry Coordinator

The youth ministry coordinator in a small youth group has the same ministry responsibilities as a youth minister in a large church—establishing a general direction for the youth ministry of the church, ministering to the needs of youth and their parents, and equipping others to minister to youth primarily through the youth program organizations.

As a member of the Youth Ministry Council, the youth ministry coordinator serves as the convener and chairperson of the Council. Because of the key role the youth ministry coordinator plays, that persons serves well in that role. This does not mean that he or she controls the meeting and that the Council has only a rubber-stamping function. What it does mean is that the youth ministry coordinator should be the best equipped, most available person in the church to coordinate such a group since he or she knows the general direction that the church's youth ministry needs to follow. The coordinator should keep the Council on track in ensuring that the activities planned have integrity and are done in a way that does not detract from the spiritual goals of the youth ministry and the church. The youth ministry coordinator can also help with the flow of Council meetings since certain personalities sometimes tend to dominate and monopolize the meetings.

The Youth Ministry Council provides an excellent avenue for the youth ministry coordinator to recognize and affirm gifts of Council members and encourage them to assume even more responsibility. Older youth have often worked in apprentice type roles with youth ministry coordinators, a role that could lead to vocational ministry.

The Planning Process

Youth Ministry Councils in smaller churches can function in all kinds of ways, but all need to accept and accomplish a few primary responsibilities and tasks.

The Council is the recognized planning group for youth programming.—Events should be planned and scheduled in Council meetings because the Council represents all youth program organizations, and conflicts can be avoided. In Council meetings calendared school events need to be considered and major conflicts avoided when possible. One goal of a Youth Ministry Council is to have balanced programming so that youth's spiritual lives are well-rounded.

The Youth Ministry Council can help plan and suggest ways needed monies can be secured and wisely spent.—If the church has a youth ministry budget, the group can assist the youth ministry coordinator in exercising good stewardship of the church's resources.

The Council can dream together about specific goals of youth ministry.—When people who care about youth ministry meet together, their collective thinking is often more likely to meet real needs and to achieve greater results.

The Youth Ministry Council serves as a think tank for recognizing other gifted people who are not on the Council.—These persons could be contacted and asked to assume leadership roles in projected programming. Having one group to delegate tasks is better than risking duplication when several groups are seeking to enlist volunteers. More people are asked to participate, and fewer people are likely to experience burnout.

Council members can encourage and support one another,

youth parents, and church leaders.—When Council members realize the magnitude of ministry responsibility, they may be overwhelmed. Mutual support and affirmation can help restore energy and vision to the task at hand. Hebrews 10:23-25 says: "Let us hold on firmly to the hope we profess, because we can trust God to keep his promise. Let us be concerned for one another, to help one another to show love and to do good. Let us not give up the habit of meeting together, as some are doing. Instead, let us encourage one another all the more, since you see that the Day of the Lord is coming nearer." (GNB).[2]

The First Steps

If the idea of a Youth Ministry Council appeals to you as youth leader in a small church, you can begin now to implement it into your youth ministry.

Pray that God will help you develop the Council in the best way for your church.—In some churches with a tradition for doing things a certain way, anything new may be questioned.

If the church already has a youth council, youth committee, or both, realize that the transition to a Youth Ministry Council may be more difficult.—Begin by sharing the idea with key people. Enlist support by explaining to them the benefits of such a Council. When the idea has been shared individually with key people (don't forget possible church bylaws that dictate standing church committees) and you feel you can proceed, meet with all youth, youth workers, and youth parents. A separate meeting for each is probably best. Meeting with adult groups (workers and parents) should precede meeting with youth in case problems arise.

After the Youth Ministry Council is approved by whatever necessary groups, enlist youth members.—No one method is right for every church. Possible ways include popular election by the entire youth group; a nomination and election process; selection by youth workers based on youth's interest, commitment, and maturity; or simply selection by application. The advantages and disadvantages of each of these plans are described in *Youth Ministry Guidebook.* Whatever plan you follow, try to ensure meaning and integrity in the process.

Select adult members of the Council.—The adult selection process is much easier because it is dictated by positions held in youth programming. Persons should be chosen to represent

Youth Sunday School, Youth Discipleship Training, missions education groups, and youth music. If some of these organizations do not currently exist in your church, ask an adult to represent that area of programming. If some of these programs are led by the same people, they would be responsible on the Council for representing both areas.

The goal in choosing Council members is balanced representation. Staying flexibly will help meet that goal.

Don't forget to include at least one parent if parents are not already represented by the youth program leaders. As a general rule, strive for equal youth and adult representation.

Once Council members are enlisted, plan an orientation retreat.—This setting is a good opportunity for the youth ministry coordinator to build a ministry team and to explore needs. Remember, retreats do not have to be overnight. They can be an all-day Saturday or a Sunday afternoon. (Again, Ross' *Youth Ministry Council Guidebook* and *Youth Ministry Council Packet* are helpful resources for planning an orientation retreat.)

After the orientation experience, whether an actual retreat or a special meeting, you are ready to begin meeting on a regular (probably monthly) basis.— The Youth Ministry Council is by no means the answer to all the problems you face in ministering to the needs of youth in a small church. However, it can provide a realistic and effective organizational approach for youth, youth parents, and youth workers to share the ministry task of fostering balanced growth among youth.

---

[1]Richard Ross, *Youth Ministry Council Guidebook* (Nashville: Convention Press, 1987).
[2]This quotation is from the *Good News Bible*, the Bible in Today's English Version. Old Testament: Copyright © American Bible Society 1976; New Testament: Copyright © American Bible Society 1966, 1971, 1986. Used by permission.

Personal Learning Activities

1. What are some benefits of having a Youth Ministry Council in a small church?

2. Who should be on the Council?

3. Why is the Youth Ministry Council the best group to plan and coordinate youth programs and activities?

4. Describe steps you would take in beginning a Youth Ministry Council.

Chapter Six

Ministering with the Parents of Youth

Jimmy Hester

Jimmy Hester is editor of Living with Teenagers, Family Ministry Department, Sunday School Board, Nashville, Tennessee.

Of the many trends emerging in Southern Baptist youth ministry, one of the most significant in the last decade has been ministry with parents of youth. As editor of *Living with Teenagers*, I often am asked to speak and lead conferences with parents of youth. My travels have taken me to large, downtown churches and fast-growing, suburban churches as well as small churches, rural and urban. My experiences lead me to conclude that the effectiveness of a ministry with parents of teenagers is not based on the number of parents involved but on a desire to address the concerns of parents. Similar issues surface whatever the size of the church.

A small church can provide an effective ministry with parents of youth. Let me illustrate by dispelling some myths about ministering with parents of youth.

Myths About Ministering with Parents of Youth

Parents don't need help; youth are the ones who need our attention and guidance.—Deep down, most parents are not as self-confident as the view expressed in this statement. Parents are searching for help. Most of them know enough about the world of their teenager to be frightened. They want to do everything possible to ensure that their teenager not only survives but also grows up to be all that God intended. Christian parents are seeking to become the best parents they can become.

If they are forced to choose, they encourage the church to devote time, money, and energy to youth instead of themselves. Parents naturally want the best for their children. But time, money, and energy invested in parents just may be what is best for their teenagers.

Churches that have been effective in making a permanent impact on the lives of youth have discovered the importance of providing for all who influence teenagers; that includes adult workers with youth, parents of youth, and youth themselves. As a youth worker in your church, you know the significance of being included in this group. Recognizing the major, permanent influence parents have on their children says something of the importance of including them in this group. We can accomplish more by working with adults and youth than we do when we work only with teenagers.

Parents of youth really don't want to be bothered with another church activity.—The assumption behind this statement is that parents are going to attend any and every activity the church schedules. Some people are present every time the doors of the church are open. Most parents of teenagers, though, are busy enough to realize that they cannot possibly attend every church activity. They become selective and invest in activities most beneficial for them and their family.

What motivates parents to attend a church activity just for them? We might learn a few things from other groups that solicit their time and energy. What does the high-school band booster club or athletic club require of parents? Most of the time they require hard work, long hours, planning, and financial support. What motivates a parent to participate? By being heavily involved, they feel that they are giving of themselves to help their teenager and the organization involved. Could the same criteria be used to plan church activities for parents that would meet their need to be a better parent and also let them recognize how they are helping their teenager and their church? Most parents will respond to a church activity if they sense it is worth the effort. If they feel it will make them a better person, and especially if they feel it will benefit their teenager, they will attend.

Some parents will support a ministry with parents of youth if they consider it an outreach ministry of the church. If the activities and projects touch the lives of parents in the community as well as those in the church, the ministry will warrant their support. And you don't have to be a large church to meet the needs of parents in your community. Families in your community need the attention that only a small church family can give.

The church is so involved with providing activities for youth that little time is left to minister with their parents.—The issue behind this statement is one of priorities. Providing an active ministry with youth is worthy. But busy schedules and full calendars don't guarantee effectiveness. For too long youth ministry in some churches has been measured by the number, rather than the quality, of activities provided. Relationships are more important than the amount of time given or the number of activities offered.

Churches involved in a ministry with parents of youth have discovered that youth activities do not have to be curtailed in order to minister with parents. Instead of discontinuing certain activities, refocusing may be a better solution. For example, instead of having a youth fellowship or a youth softball game, why not have a parent-youth fellowship or a parent-youth softball game? Instead of planning an adult mission project and a youth mission project, why not plan a parent-youth mission project?

These churches also have discovered that when they minister with parents of youth they make a strong statement to those inside and outside the church about applying the gospel message to the daily lives of teenagers and their parents.

A lot of money is required to provide a ministry with parents of youth.—As we will see in the projects and activities in the list that follows, a ministry with parents of youth does not have to be expensive. A meeting in a home with parents using a copy of *Living with Teenagers* as their discussion guide costs less than $2.00. Churches committed to providing this ministry find creative ways to provide an effective ministry with limited funds.

Using parents and other resource persons in your church is a beginning point. If your church is limited in human resources, working with another church in certain activities is an alternative. Your local Baptist association of churches is another way several churches can pool resources.

Ministering with parents of youth requires a professionally trained church staff member.—Volunteer youth workers often feel inadequate when working with parents, especially if they are parents of teenagers. Reasons include incomplete or no formal education in the area of adolescence, a lack of confidence in parenting skills, and the tension between how they parent their youth and the leadership they provide others.

"What makes me an authority in rearing youth?" they often ask. The true authority is the parent who strives daily to love, affirm, discipline, and guide his or her youth to mature, responsible Christian living.

A key word in the title of this chapter is *with*. A significant difference exists between a ministry *to* parents of youth and a ministry *with* parents of youth. *With* suggests parental involvement, while *to* suggests something given to parents.

A professionally trained church staff member is not essential to an effective ministry with parents of youth. The essential ingredients include a commitment by the church and at least one parent interested in becoming a better parent and helping others do the same.

A detailed organization is a must in providing an effective ministry with parents of youth.—Consider these statements:

- Relationships are more important than programming.
- Formal groups may or may not be necessary in providing a ministry with parents in your church.
- Detailed organization becomes critical as the size of the church grows.
- Organization is simply a tool to facilitate effective ministry.

How do these apply in your church situation? In a small church the organization of a ministry with parents may be as simple as one parent taking the lead in getting other parents together. Or a volunteer youth worker may incorporate parents in the present youth ministry.

Whoever takes the lead—whether parent, volunteer worker, or pastor—a key factor is the integration of parents in planning and promoting the projects and activities. Remember our previous discussion on what motivates parents to become active? Churches with an effective ministry with parents have found that parental involvement from the beginning is a must.

Ministry Projects with Parents of Youth

The following two lists of activities (parent-youth projects and parents supporting one another) are by no means exhaustive. A church should not attempt all of these projects in one year. Select a beginning point that will address the needs of your parents and their youth. Build on this foundation for future projects and activities. A simple project that is successful will be more valuable in the long run than a more complex project that meets with limited success.

Parent-Youth Projects

Parent-Youth Dialogue
Purpose.—To allow youth and adults to acknowledge that each has something to say and to develop skills such as talking, listening, and understanding.

Description.—Involve youth and parents in planning and promoting the dialogue. Both generations need to feel the dialogue belongs to them. As few as two youth and two parents but not more than four youth and four parents can be involved in the planning. The planning team should determine the purpose of the event and the goals the group wants to reach by conducting the dialogue. They also should determine how they will promote and conduct the dialogue.

Different experiences can be included in the dialogue event. Activities should help people initiate conversation and begin to feel comfortable talking to one another, develop listening and talking skills, and identify and discuss areas of agreement and understanding. Two examples of a parent-youth dialogue are listed. Use or adapt these and create others for use with your parents and teenagers.

Let's Talk About Curfew

Begin the dialogue by pairing off.—In this initial exercise, youth do not have to be paired with an adult. Youth can be paired with youth, and adults can be paired with adults. Make an assignment. Ask one person in each pair to respond to the other. Allow one minute. Then swap roles with the other person responding. After both have responded, have them swap partners with another pair. Repeat the exercise with a different assignment. Follow this procedure several times using the following assignments:

- Describe a funny thing that happened to you recently.
- Talk about the most influential person in your life.
- Define and react to the word *curfew*.

During the activity you may notice that youth and adults are becoming more free, more talkative, and more relaxed. If so, point this out and ask: "Why is this happening? Did anybody notice? How do you feel about talking with someone who is giving you their undivided attention?"

Select two people (a youth and an adult) to role-play a typical parent-youth conversation about establishing a curfew.—Do it with reversed roles. A youth plays the part of the parent; an adult plays the part of the teenage child. After the role play, allow plenty of time for discussion. Ask: "Was this a typical interchange between parent and teenager? Do you have a curfew at your house? How was it determined? What is a fair process for determining a curfew?"

Select two other people (a youth and an adult) to role-play a conversation between parent and child when the teenager comes in past the established curfew time.—Again, reverse the roles. After the role play, begin the discussion by asking, How typical was this conversation? What should happen when a curfew is violated? After all is said and done, what is the real reason for a curfew?

Pair off once again, this time matching teenagers with adults as much as possible.—They do not have to be from the same family although pairing them this way is OK. Give each pair seven minutes to develop a curfew that is acceptable to both parent and teenager. If you have parents in the group who consider the subject nonnegotiable, encourage them to try the exercise anyway. After they have completed their work, allow time for each pair to share their plan. You may want to compile these into one list that will give several alternatives to establishing curfew. Encourage parents and teenagers to take the list home and discuss it further as a family.

Let's Talk About Money

Begin this dialogue just like the one above.—Some other assignments you can make include:

- Talk about what you like best about yourself.
- Describe your idea of a happy family.
- Describe what you would do with $100.

Remember to discuss how participants feel about the dialogue that is taking place.

Form a panel of two youth and two adults.—They are to be the experts on parents, teenagers, and money. The remaining parents and youth will direct questions to these four people. The four are to respond openly and honestly, representing their age group. To get the discussion started, plant a couple of questions in the audience, such as:

- Should a teenager receive an allowance?
- How should the amount of allowance be determined?
- Is an allowance something that should be earned or is it a gift?
- What should an allowance include (church offering, clothing, recreation, etc.?)
- Should a teenager have a checking account? credit cards?

Pair off matching adults and youth, as in the first exercise.— In this exercise give each pair seven minutes to develop a plan for allowances that is acceptable to both parent and teenager.

Parent-Youth Bible Study

Purpose.—To reinforce a teenager's Bible study experience in Sunday School and to offer parent and youth an opportunity for joint Bible study and relationship building.

Description.—"Home Encounters with the Bible" is an ongoing feature in *Living with Teenagers* magazine. Parents are encouraged to review and select material that corresponds to the Bible study series (Convention Uniform, Life and Work, and

Bible Book) their teenager uses in Sunday School. *Living with Teenagers* provides suggested activities for one Sunday School lesson per month per Bible study series. Parents are asked to read with their teenager the suggested activities and decide together how to do them.

The suggested methods imply a relaxed atmosphere where parents and youth can communicate openly. Parents using "Home Encounters with the Bible" have found many opportunities to discuss a variety of topics and to build stronger relationships with their youth.

Parent-Youth Recreation/Fellowship Activities

Purpose.—To deepen parent-teen relationships through fellowship, play, and recreation.

Description.—Some of my fondest teenage memories of times with my dad were church softball games. Fathers and sons sometimes played on the same team; other times they played against each other. Not only did we have fun and get some exercise, but we also received something much more valuable—a deeper understanding of each other and a closer relationship.

Just about any recreational activity that has been planned for youth can include adults. Softball, volleyball, hiking, basketball, and many other activities are popular activities among parents and teenagers.

Along with recreation parent-youth fellowships provide wonderful opportunities for fun and games. You can create many an enjoyable evening by challenging a parent and a teenager to plan a fellowship for parents and youth in the church. By rotating the planning, a variety of fun-filled evenings will emerge.

Here is one idea to get you started. Materials needed include a dictionary, pencils, and paper. Pair off, preferably with a parent and youth in each pair. Select a pair to begin and then rotate the assignment with the other pairs. The assignment is to select a word in the dictionary they think no one else in the room will be able to define. They are given two minutes to select a word. They are to pronounce the word for everyone to hear, spell it, and pronounce it a second time. At this point, each pair is given five minutes to come up with a definition. The definition is to be written on a piece of paper and given to the pair who selected the word. One of them reads the definitions submitted and allows the group to agree on one definition.

This becomes the preferred definition. The question is, Is it the right definition? In most cases it probably is not, but the difference in the perceived definition and the real one is a lot of fun. After the definitions are compared and the laughter dies down, repeat the process with a new pair selecting a word.

Parent-Youth Day

Purpose.—To focus the attention of the church on parent-youth relationships and to offer opportunities for parents and youth to strengthen that relationship.

Description.—A Sunday devoted to highlighting parent-youth relationships can be as simple or as complex as you want to make it. The day can include many activities or a couple of activities. Pick the items from the following list which are best suited for your church.

• Parent-youth-worker reception.—Begin the day with a reception 20 minutes prior to Sunday School for parents and their youth and the volunteer youth workers. Serve light refreshments, and allow plenty of time for informal conversation. Even if your church is small and everyone knows everyone else, this gives an opportunity not often afforded for youth workers, parents, and youth to focus on their relationships. If your church reaches youth whose parents do not attend regularly, a personal invitation should be extended to encourage their participation.

• Worship.—Include parents and their youth in worship services during the day. Parent-youth testimonies, duets, and prayers are possibilities. The pastor may want to preach a sermon on the Christian home.

• Luncheon.—A covered-dish luncheon for parents and their youth followed by a recreational activity allows for a time of fellowship and fun. Keep it simple. The focus is on building relationships not on fancy food.

• Parent-youth fellowship.—Consider the ideas under "Parent-Youth Recreation/Fellowship" for a parent-youth fellowship after the evening worship service, or create your own.

Parent-Youth Mission Projects

Purpose.—To meet a specific need by ministering to others through a mission project and to unite the parents and their teenagers in a common cause.

Description.—Parent-youth mission projects can be as simple as assisting an elderly neighbor with household chores or as elaborate as traveling to a resort area and conducting a mini-drama. These projects can be done by groups of families or by an individual family. Space does not allow a comprehensive listing and description of possible parent-youth mission projects. Without giving details, a few possible target groups might include elderly persons inside and outside the church, physically handicapped children, blind persons, international college students, hospital patients, or vacationers. If a family decides to take on an involved project, other parents and their teenagers in the church might become sponsors.

Family Swap

Purpose.—To cause parents and teenagers to consider new ideas about family living.

Description.—In a family swap parents exchanging teenagers for a weekend. Follow two guidelines in making assignments: (1) Place youth in a home with a teenager of the same sex and, if possible, similar age. This provides a comfortable beginning for everyone. (2) A direct swap is not necessary. If my teenager goes to your house, your teenager does not necessarily have to come to mine. I may end up with someone else's youth.

Launch the weekend with a Saturday morning breakfast and orientation at the church, the home of a church member, or a local restaurant. Cover the ground rules such as: watch little or no television, do not contact any of the other families during the away-from-church times, and have fun!

The weekend should involve parents and teenagers doing something fun together with their new family on Saturday, attending Sunday morning activities together and sitting as a new family in the worship service, and coming together on Sunday afternoon or evening for an evaluation session with all families included. In the evaluation session allow both generations to share their experiences and insights.

Parents Supporting One Another

Parents' Roundtable

Purpose.—To allow parents to recognize that similar issues are faced in every family, to provide a forum for parents to share workable solutions to family issues, and to provide parents mutual support in an affirming environment.

Description.—A parents' roundtable may be a one-time project or a monthly or quarterly activity. A youth leader or parent can serve as moderator. The moderator's role is to keep the spirit of the discussion affirming and healthy, move to another question at the appropriate time, and help parents realize they do not have to reach a consensus. Sometimes a question has no right answer, and the moderator should avoid giving what is perceived as the right answer.

The roundtable can be conducted at the church or in a home. It begins with a time of informal fellowship. After parents begin to feel comfortable with one another, the moderator gives each parent a piece of paper to write anonymous questions to be answered by the entire group. The moderator asks one question at a time, allowing the group to struggle with each question.

The interesting thing about a parents' roundtable is that each session is different. Different parents usually attend; different questions are asked; different responses are made based on recent experiences.

Parents' Support Activities
Purpose.—To encourage, nurture, and sustain the ongoing growth of parents and to help parents develop close relationships with other parents who value healthy Christian family life.

Description.—A parents' support group may consist of any number of parents. Parents may choose to meet in a member's home or at church. Parents meet to encourage one another in the growth and enrichment of their parenting skills.

If individuals or couples wish to use this approach to parent enrichment for private home study, they need to determine that this study is something they want to do, pray that God will open new growth opportunities, decide on a consistent place and time, and obtain a copy of *Living with Teenagers* and use the "Parents: Sharing and Supporting" feature.

If more than two parents want to form a group for a regular support time, one parent can take the initiative and enlist other parents of youth. Follow the guidelines listed in the preceding paragraph to get the group organized. The most effective parent support groups include both fathers and mothers. Some groups, though, are only mothers or fathers. One group of fathers in a church in Texas meets monthly for breakfast.

"Parents: Sharing and Supporting" is a regular feature in *Living with Teenagers* magazine. It helps parents discover new insights regarding parenting concerns, affirm one another's gifts and strengths, and assist in strengthening one another's families. Each segment (one for each month in the quarter) introduces a parental concern, offers a solution, and contains open-ended questions to help parents explore options.

Parenting by Grace

Purpose.—To help churches grow parents in the Christian faith and in skills to help them lead their teenagers to Christian maturity and to help parents use the gift of God's grace as they love, affirm, discipline, and guide their teenagers to mature, responsible Christian living.

Description.—Parenting by Grace, part of the LIFE learning system of Discipleship Training, is a course of study that could be the biggest, most challenging parent event of the year. Even so, it may be the most rewarding experience of the year.

A Parenting by Grace course is arranged into units of study; units are divided into lessons. Each participant completes a directed study plan for each lesson prior to a weekly group meeting. Group size is recommended to be 4-16 parents. Each group should schedule a weekly, one- to two-hour session facilitated by one of the parents. Each parent has a workbook, and the facilitator has a leader's notebook.

In addition to the lessons is a one-hour introductory session. The introductory material contains an overview, introduction, and foundation to Parenting by Grace; commitment to participate; and take-home assignments.

Parenting by Grace will contain several courses that address key parent concerns. The first course is on discipline and spiritual growth. Units of study include:
- Grace: God's Gift to Parents and Children
- Helping Children Grow According to God's Plan
- How to Discipline by Grace
- Applying Grace to Your Parenting
- Sustaining Grace in Your Parenting

A second course, dealing with self-esteem, is scheduled for release in October 1991.

Projects with Other Churches

Every project and activity suggested in this chapter was selected with the small church in mind. Some are easier to provide than others, but all are within the means of most small churches.

Several small churches may want to pool their resources and make a greater impact on the communities they serve by joining hands on a project or activity. Not only could the churches reach out to the community, but the cooperation between the parents and youth of several churches could broaden the perspective of parents and youth in your church.

Resources

The following items are available from Customer Service Center, 127 Ninth Avenue, North, Nashville, TN 37234, (toll free 1-800-458-BSSB, 7:30 am-4:00 pm, CST, Monday-Friday) or the Baptist Book Store serving you.

Hauk, Gary H. *Family Enrichment in Your Church*. Nashville: Convention Press, 1988.

Living with Teenagers. Quarterly magazine for parents of youth published by the Family Ministry Department, Baptist Sunday School Board, Nashville, TN.

Parenting by Grace: Discipline and Spiritual Growth. Parent's Guide and Leader's Notebook. Published by the Family Ministry and Discipleship Training Departments, Baptist Sunday School Board, Nashville, TN.

Ross, Richard, compiler. *Successes in Southern Baptist Youth Ministry*. Nashville: Convention Press, 1988.

Ross, Richard. *Youth Ministry Planbook 4*. Nashville: Convention Press, 1989.

Ross, Richard and G. Wade Rowatt, Jr. *Ministry with Youth and Their Parents*. Nashville: Convention Press, 1986.

Personal Learning Activities

1. Discuss several myths about ministering with parents of youth, and explain why they are not true.

2. Discuss two projects your church could use to minister to parents.

Chapter Seven

Promoting Youth Ministry

Irene Bennett

Irene Bennett is minister of education, First Baptist Church, Evans, Georgia.

"This tape sounds just like a television commercial!" complained Jeremy.

"Exactly," chorused Lynn and David. "We want it to make people want to do this musical."

The three senior-high youth worked together to produce a cassette tape to mail to all the youth in the church. They put the finishing touches on a wrapper for each tape and addressed the mailers. A large neighboring church duplicated the tapes on the equipment normally used for sermon tapes. For about 75 cents each, 30 youth received an unusual and personal invitation to begin rehearsal for a youth musical.

"Enthusiasm is contagious."

"Success breeds success."

"A good youth program will sell itself."

Truisms? Maybe. Whatever the quality of youth ministry in your church and however you or your teenagers or church members feel about it, people do have impressions about what is going on. To set out deliberately to shape those impressions for specific purposes is to promote your youth ministry.

What Are Promotion, Publicity, and Public Relations?

Exactly what constitutes promotion? Why promote your youth ministry? To whom and by whom is promotion done? How do you promote youth ministry? Consider the suggestions in this chapter as springboards for designing your unique approach to promotion. Everything mentioned here cannot and need not be done in one place or in one year. Each youth ministry needs to seek a balanced approach that works well for each year. Promotion includes advertising, publicity, and public relations as a whole. Advertising usually involves paying for time or space in order to distribute information about your youth ministry. It calls attention to your total program or particular events through such media as newspaper ads, billboards, signs, radio or television commercials. Basically advertising creates awareness of and interest in your youth ministry.

Publicity includes numerous ways of sharing newsworthy information about immediate events with the church and the community. Examples of publicity include press releases, community service announcements on radio or television, interviews on community programs produced locally, mailouts, announcements, posters, signs, flyers, bulletin boards, telephone chains or blitzes, balloons, tickets, handouts, tapes, free gifts. While advertising and publicity are among the tools of communication, public relations encompasses everything that represents your youth ministry to whomever observes it or takes part in it.

The first two forms of promotion, advertising and publicity, ordinarily focus on sharing information about the total ministry, about regularly planned programming, or about special events. Usually they aim at particular persons whom you want to participate in or to support given programs or events. Public relations, on the other hand, intends to create or to maintain good relationships between each of your publics and your youth ministry. It creates an image about the kind of youth ministry you have; or it presents the purposes or goals of the total ministry, particular programs, or specific events. It is often relational in that public relations uses a variety of methods to create and maintain relationships among the church and youth and their families and other adults in the church and in the community.

Public relations can include repetitive use of such means as logos or themes, speeches to church or community groups, participation in or leadership of churchwide or community events, sponsorship of churchwide or community events, ministry to and with other groups, videotape or slide presentations, reports to relevant groups. In a world inundated with promotional messages for everything, you must become informed about and intentional in your use of the most effective means of telling the good news about your youth ministry. Begin by adopting an open-eyed, "what if" mentality about the possibilities, and be creative where you are. Many options are available in even the smallest church setting.

Who Promotes Your Youth Ministry?

First, who plans and carries out the promotion of the youth ministry? The most available and knowledgeable person or persons work best. The staff member or volunteer leader responsible for the youth ministry may have the most information, time, and know-how. Or a parent or one or more volunteers can make contributions in this area, but the key youth leader still needs to facilitate the process. A team of helpers can be enlisted so the person responsible does not work alone.

Someone in the church with experience in desktop publishing may design layouts for newspaper ads, newsletters, logos, and flyers. Others may write or type well, make posters or create bulletin boards. Some teenagers love making photos or producing audio or videotapes with their own equipment. Enlisting volunteers spreads the work load and the joy of service and is in itself a form of promotion.

One person should develop relationships with persons at local newspapers and radio and television stations who write or edit religious or community news. Learning their schedules and format requirements for news will enable you to give them information in the most usable form. In addition to press releases, the youth leader with writing skills might try writing for the "Teen Scene" section or the editorial page of the local paper. Local media personnel want to know about happenings that they consider to be newsworthy—that is, of community interest. They also like working with persons who understand their needs and present them with material that does not need rewriting.

Likewise, Southern Baptist agencies have support personnel for youth ministry who want to develop relationships with key youth leaders in every church. The Baptist Sunday School Board programming and support sections—Sunday School, Discipleship Training, Church Music, Church Recreation, Church Administration—all want to communicate directly with you about products and services they can provide you. They also want to hear about what you do with your teenagers that works. The same is true of the Woman's Missionary Union and the Brotherhood Commission and the state convention offices. Ask your pastor to share with you the information about youth ministry that he receives from these support people. He or your associational director of missions can help you contact any of these persons.

Also be certain that the name of the key youth leader appears on the Uniform Church Letter that your church clerk or secretary completes by September 30 each year. Most of the agencies mail information about youth ministry to that person which helps with programming and promotion.

The person who does promotion for several years becomes proficient at it. Helping someone to grow in this area, even if it is himself, should be one goal of the youth ministry coordinator. With the right person in charge, the right approach to promotion can be developed. Key people decide why specific promotion is needed; what the message is; to whom, how, and when to say it; and finally how well you have said it.

Why Do You Need to Promote Your Youth Ministry?
Purposes for promotion have to do with a sense of self as a total ministry and goals for particular activities. Who are we and what do we hope to be? What do we want to be known for? Active youth, parents, and workers with youth might want to discuss possible answers to such identity questions. Not only does the process help to create a self-concept for your youth ministry, but it will also clarify purposes for different parts of the

ministry. From this sense of self, ongoing themes and logos can be developed for repeated use in promotion. A youth group might want to emphasize its family qualities by describing itself as, "The Church Where Everyone Counts" or "When You're Absent, Someone Notices," or "The Caring Crowd in the Heart of Downtown," or "Funny, Friendly, and Faithful— That's Us!"

What do we want to result from a particular event or program we have planned? Specific goals for activities produce specific promotion purposes. Promotion for a retreat to improve witnessing skills would have a different purpose than that for a community-wide seminar or concert. The former would be designed to appeal to the desire of active teenagers in the church who want to share their faith, while the latter would be designed to use the concern of parents about dating or the music interest of unchurched youth in the community to attract them to a seminar or a Christian concert.

The purpose of the event and therefore of the promotion will affect the language and content of the message. The central idea must be clear and meaningful to the persons you want to reach. The promoter must answer some basic questions: Why would the listener, viewer, or reader be interested in this objective? Which words or pictures will communicate best with him or her? How can we honestly and concisely express our message?

Purposes also determine target audiences for promotion. The youth ministry has several publics—active teenagers and their families, the congregation, and unreached teenagers in the community. For example, promotion aimed at parents of younger, active youth may emphasize that their support will provide a sound youth ministry for their young people. On the other hand, promotion aimed at the congregation as a whole may point out the vitality and ministry opportunity that a youth program can give the church. Promotion to unreached teenagers in the community might appeal to their desire for friends, for personal improvement, for helpingothers, or for wholesome entertainment.

Ongoing promotion to active teenagers not only encourages participation but also creates an informed core of supporters and promoters or PR persons. Periodic promotion to the congregation informs them, enlists their support, and invites the inactive teenager to take part. Advertising or publicity directed to the general public calls short-lived attention to the youth ministry, while efforts that build relationships inside and outside the church tend to influence long-lasting attitudes.

How Do You Promote Your Youth Ministry?

Leaders in communications often say: "Tell people that you are going to tell them something. Tell them what you want them to know. Then tell them that you have told them!" This simple idea translates into a basic rule of thumb for a minimum publicity strategy: three weeks, three kinds, three audiences.

To promote an upcoming event requires at least three weeks lead time. Since 50 percent average attendance is the national norm for Southern Baptist Sunday Schools, most people probably attend about two Sundays per month. So, if your Sunday publicity covers three weeks, the regular attenders should see or hear it at least once. Repeating information on Sunday or in the church's weekly mailout for at least three weeks reinforces the message for your members.

Research about learning styles demonstrates that people differ in the kind of messages which appeal to them or to which they respond. Also, researchers tell us that people remember information better when data comes to them through more than one sense at the same time. Usually in sharing information we employ oral means first, written messages second, visual aids third, and tasting or touching methods rarely if ever. The more the target audience can participate in the publicity event the more likely they are to remember the message. So, if at least three different methods are used to publicize the same event, more people should get the message.

Three audiences almost always go together when publicizing an event for teenagers—the youth, their parents, and the church family. The same information about a certain event may be presented in different ways to each group. Publicity for the teenagers informs and invites; for the parents and the church it informs and explains purposes. Of course, three sets of teenagers interest us, too—active youth, inactive youth, and community youth or prospects. Again, the audience dictates the message and/or its medium.

In 1988, businesses in the United States spent $103.5 billion promoting their products and services—34 percent at meetings and conventions, 16 percent at point of purchase; 16 percent in incentives; 10 percent in advertising; the remaining 24 percent in varied ways.[1] Assuming that a similar division of effort would be effective with promoting a youth ministry, then one third of youth promotion should be where teenagers and/or parents gather, one third should be during youth programs or activities and should include incentives, and the last third should be advertising and miscellaneous efforts.

Promotion at church during Youth Sunday School, Discipleship Training, missions education meetings, choir rehearsals, and worship may seem obvious; but it must be done well and continually. And have you thought of promoting one youth event at another? Publicity about youth activities also needs to be shared at classes or meetings attended by parents of youth.

Incentives.—Consider adding tangible incentives as well as pointing out the intangible benefits of participation. Free tickets for active youth to give away to others, recognition and affirmation for a job well-done, special gifts for the first five youth who commit to go to Centrifuge or Crosspoint, or an extra game of miniature golf for the youth who brings the most members to Youth Vacation Bible School are just a few simple examples of incentives.

Incentives consistent with the kinds of attitudes or behaviors you are trying to encourage are more effective than just any material or financial reward for winning some competition. Give away copies of *Living with Teenagers* or *event!* magazine at gatherings of parents or youth in your community. Attach a label that says, "a gift from Local Baptist Church, the church that cares about teenagers." Or present a card with the magazine that invites, "For more information, call Local Baptist Church." Insert a flyer about the next activity for youth or parents being sponsored by your church, or include a weekly schedule of youth events. Put them in public lobbies, doctors' waiting rooms, laundromats, car washes, beauty shops, community center lounges, apartment complex or mobile home recreation rooms—wherever someone might read while waiting on something else. Of course, in all of the above places, ask permission of the manager or other person in charge first. And regularly return to remove old issues and leave the latest ones.

Advertising.—Advertising reaches a large audience with a particular message usually for a special event of interest to the community—youth-led revivals, VBS for youth, special speaker or performer of interest to both churched and unchurched youth, introduction of the ministry at the beginning of the school year or of the summer. Newspapers, signs, radio, and television sell space or time for advertising. Choose the medium, day, and time that the audience you want will be exposed to the message. Budget requirements may dictate limited but wise use of advertising.

Personal contact.—Many possibilities for promotion exist in every situation. Choosing the most appropriate medium depends on the target audience and cost. Direct contact or word of mouth remains the most effective, least expensive form of promotion. Friends believe what friends or people they trust tell them. For active teenagers and their families, a calendar, newssheet, or newsletter helps this process. Because of their commitment and participation, they want basic details about youth events. They must have accurate information to share with friends. Articles in the weekly mailout or the Sunday bulletin keep them, the church family, informed and able to share with the people they know about youth ministry plans.

Telephone chains or blitzes by active youth to youth or parents to parents provide an invaluable personal touch through a favorite instrument. And it is even better when the youth can go by a teenager's house to say: "The church youth group is playing softball (going to the movie or to get pizza or over to the Joneses for the evening). Will you go with us?" If the youth declines, then the visitors invite him or her to Sunday School and leave some youth material. Some churches regularly schedule such organized activities because they often reach inactive youth this way.

Announcement periods in classes or in Sunday or Wednesday night worship can be personal also in that they are person-to-group experiences. They can be simple or sophisticated and may be done by a youth or an adult. Simple invitations, monologues, skits, puppets, hidden tape recordings, a single slide with a brief paragraph, someone carrying an object or dressed in clothes associated with an event and mingling with early arrivers or seated in the group—all briefly but personally convey a message to youth or their parents. These same means may also be used at any youth event to promote another event.

Personal contact can also be made with groups in the church

or the community. Speaking about a youth ministry project or mission trip to a senior-adult meeting or a WMU or Brotherhood group gives them details and presents ways they can be supportive. If your youth group leads in or decides as a group to support a neighborhood clean-up campaign, a cemetery restoration project, a bike-a-thon for world hunger, or any drive with which the community can identify, local school or civic groups may welcome a speaker on the subject. How about establishing a youth speakers bureau? Two or three youth or adult volunteers can prepare to talk about certain aspects of your ministry. Just let the appropriate people in the church or community know they are available. Likewise, invite school, business, or other community personnel to address youth or adults at the church on such topics as handling crises, teenagers on the job, or county recreation and the church.

Church conference or business meeting provides a unique moment for promotion with a personal feature. Members of the congregation like to hear healthy statistics, but the bottom line for them is more often personal success stories or evidence that the youth ministry is working. Share spiritual decisions made by youth that month at church or after a revival, retreat, VBS, camp, or choir tour—professions of faith, rededications, commitment to missions service or vocational ministry. Even if these decisions were made publicly, some church members will not know about them. Point out youth activities that indicate growth—youth-led events or projects or renewed interest in choir or missions groups, for example. Ask a teenager, a parent, or a youth leader to give a testimony about how God is at work in his or her life. Introduce the honor camper or the soloists for the youth choir presentation or the players in the Easter drama. People talking to people is promotion, and it is ministry.

Printed materials.—Newssheets or newsletters and calendars are most commonly used because they provide regular communication with all members. Computer software is available to assist in designing both. Clip art for newsletters and calendars can be found in *equipping youth*, Baptist Book Stores, or other bookstores or office supply stores. Using duplicating and copy machines is less costly for a small number of copies than printing; and newsletters reproduced this way can look good.

Decisions must also be made about frequency, content, production, and distribution. If a lot is happening quickly, members may need a newssheet or newsletter weekly or a calendar monthly; otherwise, they may be distributed quarterly or seasonally, for example, at the beginning of the school year or the summer. They may vary in length and content, but they should tell readers what is going on and who is involved. Successes, recognitions, birthdays, publicity for activities, requests for volunteers, along with regular features such as a youth leader's column, Youth Ministry Council report, or letters from readers provide both freshness and continuity in a newsletter.

Newsletters and calendars can be given to active youth at church, inserted in the bulletin or weekly mailout to the entire congregation, or mailed to youth. Even in small situations enough copies may be mailed to use the bulk rate for postage; if not, third class is an option when fast delivery is not required. Newsletters and calendars attract the inactive or prospective youth member and their parents and encourage participation of the active, so they are effective in all but quite small, tightly knit groups with very limited programming.

Posters are the simplest form of display and may be used for any target audience—teenagers, parents, church family, or community. Effective posters can be produced inexpensively by youth or adults. Since posters abound and people read them as they pass by, they must be attention getting, brief, and clear with easily read lettering and only a few colors, images, or words. Place them in key places where people are most likely to see them and remove them promptly when the event is over.

A set of posters for a youth-led revival might go something like this: In youth classrooms, "We Need *You* in the *You*th-Led Revival." In parents' classrooms, "The Youth-Led Revival Needs Your Teenager." In the church hallway "Support Your Teenagers with Your Prayers and Presence." On school locker doors of active youth, "Follow the Crowd to Services of Youth, by Youth, and for Youth." And in places of business near the church, "Tomorrow's Leaders Lead Today! Attend the Youth-Led Revival at Local Baptist Church."

A youth handbook can be a vital part of youth communication. Include names of teenagers by grades, their parents' names, addresses, telephone numbers, and the teenagers' birthdays as well as church policies that affect youth programming or participation. It will help youth, parents, and leaders stay in touch with one another and new members to become acquainted with others.

A calendar, even if incomplete, gives readers a feel for the ministry through an overview of a year's plans.

Direct mail probably follows oral announcements as a popular choice for promotion. Birthday cards, get-well wishes, and thank-you notes are essential ingredients in letting youth know someone cares. Preprinted cards or postcards become special with a handwritten note. Such individual attention promotes the interest of the youth in the church.

Flyers and invitations, brochures and reminders may also be mailed to a large number of youth without an envelope and at lower rates than a first-class letter. Ask your postmaster to explain the possibilities. Anything sent through the mail needs to be attention getting, readable, and attractive. The key point needs to be obvious and may need to be repeated. A mailing list of members and prospects needs to be kept up-to-date by putting "address correction requested" on a mailout once or twice a year. The post office charges a small fee for this service, but it is worth it.

A youth information rack, table, or shelf should always have extra copies of flyers, handouts, or mailouts. It needs to be in a high-traffic area for youth and their parents, so they can get information when they have lost or forgotten it.

Printing free tickets for an event and having active youth give them to inactive youth or youth in the community combines print and personal communication. Giving a prospect a free dinner-with-the-minister coupon is another way to use printed material to present an image of your ministry.

Cameras, cassette recorders, camcorders, and telephone answering machines enhance promotion by providing messages in an unusual or unexpected way. Church members often own such equipment and are delighted to use it for the church.

Youth bulletin boards, a youth annual complete with snapshots, and slide shows of youth activities are all possible outcomes of a roving photographer's work which both teenagers and the congregation can enjoy. A "We're Going Again!" bulletin board could feature snapshots and statements of youth who plan to go to camp for the second time. Or, how about an "I Was 'Snickered' Last Wednesday Night" Bible study photo lineup with candy-bar-wrapper accents?

Cassette recorders and camcorders can be used for "person

on the street" interviews or to prepare a youth "news scene" for an announcement period. Or ask school officials if you may tape a local ball game and ask the manager of a local youth hangout if you may show the tape there after the game that night. Then, during halftime pass out free tickets to the "Instant Replay" sponsored by Local Baptist Church youth group.

Place an answering machine on the church telephone at certain times of the day to serve as a youth ministry hotline. Youth can record an entertaining message giving the details of upcoming events. Print business cards with the hotline number,and give them to active youth to distribute indiscriminately. Such an information service can promote youth ministry to youth, parents, church members, and community youth.

Specialty items with custom imprints such as banners, balloons, bumper stickers, buttons, T-shirts, sun visors, caps, and jackets are forms of promotion that can be used within the congregation or in the community. Some can be used over a long period of time, so the original expense is worth it; others may need to be reserved for special events. Such items heighten name recognition or increase awareness of a coming event.

Some of the most welcome words a youth leader hears from newcomers or others in the community are, "I hear you have a good youth program." He or she knows that satisfied, informed youth and church members are telling friends and neighbors and people they meet about the church's ministry. Having people think well of your church's youth ministry is a direct result of quality programming and effective promotion.

---

[1]"Market Report," *The Augusta Chronicle*, 1 July 1989, Business section, p. 6B, col. 1.

Personal Learning Activities

1. Who are your audiences?

2. What methods of promotion are you already using effectively?

3. What methods can you begin to use and how will you use them to their best advantage?

Chapter Eight

Financing Youth Ministry

Judi S. Hayes

Judi S. Hayes is a design editor, Church Administration Department, Sunday School Board, Nashville, Tennesee.

Financing youth ministry may be the baggage that goes with an otherwise enjoyable ministry! Most youth ministry coordinators do not enjoy budgeting or trying to decide how to pay for youth ministry activities beyond the limits of the budget. All churches must be concerned with this issue, but perhaps in a small youth group it takes on added dimensions.

In a large church or large youth group, few events or activities include total youth participation. So if a youth can't afford to go on a ski trip, maybe no one notices. And many youth will likely elect not to go on such a trip, so one person's absence is not so apparent. But in a small youth group almost all youth tend to participate in nearly every event. No one would want any youth to be excluded for financial reasons. And if a youth didn't participate because of lack of funds, many people would probably know.

Because youth ministry coordinators do not want to exclude anyone who may not have enough money for youth activities and because they do not know what to do about it, they may simply limit the number of youth events planned. But steps can be taken and plans made to balance activities so that no family must face financial strain for their youth to be active in youth activities and events.

Begin with a Budget
Many youth ministry coordinators may never have had any opportunity to impact the church's budget. They simply try to work within a specified amount approved by the church each year. Perhaps no one knows the source or the reason for the amount designated for youth. The amount may have been carried over or nominally increased from year to year. Or perhaps no money is specifically budgeted for youth events.

The place to start is with a planned budget request. Rather than simply asking for a specific amount, the youth ministry coordinator should present an itemized plan for spending. Ideally each event should be listed with a purpose, a sponsoring program organization, a proposed date, and a dollar figure. Of course, to do this the youth ministry coordinator should work with the Youth Ministry Council to plan a year's activities based on goals derived from perceived needs. More information about that planning process can be found in chapter 5.

This type of budget planning is often called Ministry Action Budgeting. The Stewardship Commission has available more information about how to prepare a budget using this process. A sample budget using a planning process based on ministry needs might be something like the one on the next page.

Youth Ministry Budget

Goal Action	Organization	Amount	Date
Goal 1—To begin Youth Discipleship Training and to have half of those actively involved in Sunday School attending Youth Discipleship Training by September 30.			
• Promote Youth Discipleship Training in Sunday School.	Discipleship Training	$000	January
• Have Youth Discipleship retreat.	Discipleship Training	200	April
• Provide snack for youth on Sunday night.	Discipleship Training	000	ongoing
Goal 2—To train Youth Sunday School workers.			
• Take Youth Sunday School teachers to associational Sunday School training conferences.	Sunday School	000	October
• Begin having weekly workers meetings on Wednesday nights.	Sunday School	000	ongoing
• Train Youth Sunday School workers by using Church Study Course books.	Discipleship Training	000	ongoing
• Have a banquet for all youth workers. Recognize Sunday School workers who have earned a CSC diploma.	all programs	75	September
Goal 3—To provide opportunities for youth to learn about missions and to participate in mission activities.			
• Teach the foreign mission book at a member's home on a Saturday. Include a meal featuring foods from that country.	Missions Education Organizations	25	December
• Sponsor a Parents' Night Out during the Christmas season. Donated funds for babysitting go to Lottie Moon.	Missions Educations Organizations	10	December
• Work with local Big Brothers organization to pack and deliver food to needy families.	Missions Education Organizations	0	November
• Visit local nursing homes and church shut-ins and take homemade Valentines.	Missions Education Organizations	0	February
• Guide youth in providing help for the church's children's VBS.	Sunday School	0	June
Goal 4—To encourage youth to bring friends to church with them.			
• Have a different activity each quarter where admission price is bringing a visitor.	all organizations	100	ongoing
Goal 5—To encourage youth involvement and leadership in the church.			
• Have the Youth Choir sing at least once per quarter.	Youth Choir	0	ongoing
• Involve youth in worship at least once a month in worship by having them read Scripture, sing, pray, provide drama, etc.	all organizations	0	ongoing
• Involve all youth in a leadership role during Youth Week.	Discipleship Training	0	March
	TOTAL	$410	

This budget, of course, does not include literature for the program organizations. Other activities all may come from the recreation budget.

In this example youth are involved in a variety of experiences throughout the year. All have a purpose, but many cost nothing. The snack suppers on Sunday night, for example, can be provided by adults who volunteer on a rotating basis. An option would be to budget money for this item.

Consider Fund-Raising

Sometimes a youth group will want to raise money for any number of expenditures beyond a normal, budgeted amount. The youth may want to take a mission trip to another state. They may want to donate a new dishwasher to the church kitchen. They may want to refurbish the youth rooms or to purchase recreation equipment.

Youth and their leaders may have many good reasons for needing nonbudgeted monies; but before planning the church's first bake sale, a youth ministry coordinator should understand specifically the church's policies and opinions about fund-raising. In some churches members will support almost any activity youth want to attempt. Other churches would not consider receiving any money except through offerings.

The youth ministry coordinator may check church policy and find nothing about fund-raising. So the pastor is the next source of information. He may think it's OK. But that casual permission should not necessarily be seen as a green light. More consensus may be needed before attempting a project of this nature. The Church Council may be the most appropriate group in which to explore such a new idea.

Activities for earning money vary widely. A few categories include:

In-church activities.—These are activities that take place at the church such as bake sales or spaghetti suppers.

Away-from-church activities.—These activities are group projects, such as car washes, created by the youth group to earn money.

Business support.—In these projects youth groups work with local businesses to perform contract labor such as stuffing envelopes or distributing flyers.

Individual activities.—Youth work alone or in small groups in various tasks of their choice to earn money. A certain percentage or all of the money goes toward the project goal. Tasks may include baby-sitting, housecleaning, yard work, etc.

The method of raising money is important. Persons who say they are against money-raising activities may have particular kinds of activities in mind. Those who are against selling candy bars at church may approve of having a car wash at the bank down the street. Members who do not approve of paying youth to paint a shut-in's house might support youth washing cars for a used-car dealer. Some who do not approve of a fund-raiser for a ski trip may think it's a great idea for a mission trip.

Before attempting any kind of activity to earn money for a youth project or presenting the idea to the Church Council, the youth ministry coordinator should be prepared to answer these questions:

Why do the youth need the money? How much money is needed? Why was this project not included in the budget?—Monies received from fund-raisers are best used for one-time events such as to go on a mission trip or to purchase a dishwasher or for mission projects such as a Lottie Moon Christmas Offering. Ongoing operating expenses for youth ministry probably should be budgeted.

How much money will be earned from this activity? How will it be used? Who will benefit from the project?—The answers to these questions should help determine whether enough money can be earned to make the project worthwhile. If youth will not earn much money, will they learn anything from the activity itself? If the money is for a trip, will the money go into a pool for everyone going on a trip or only for those who participate in this event? If some youth participate in fund-raising events and others do not, will their expenses for the trip be the same or will they vary depending on their involvement in fund-raising events?

Should this activity be a mission project instead of a fundraiser?—If youth are being paid by church members to do chores, how will youth respond to helping needy members who cannot afford to pay? How will leaders help youth differentiate between fund-raisers and mission actions?

Would another way of obtaining the money be preferable?—Are some members uncomfortable with the fund-raising activity? What will youth learn from the activity? Would the church prefer a special offering, private donations, or perhaps a different kind of fund-raising activity?

With the Church Council's blessing and a clear goal in mind, the next step is to plan the details of the fund-raising event. With careful planning youth can learn something from the event, have a great time, and raise money for their goal.

Considering some guidelines could improve any fund-raising event:

• Choose activities that will maximize income and persons involved.

• Make it a church event rather than a youth event.

• Include as many people as possible.

• Look for ways to include fringe youth.

• Promote the event as widely as possible for several weeks prior to the event.

• Keep expenses for the event down by asking members to donate materials needed.

• Discover ways to multiply the income for a single event.

Unique opportunities are available for any youth group. Church members may have great ideas from their businesses for youth projects. For example, one youth group washed airplanes for a local airport. Another group of youth spent a day pretending to be disaster victims for the National Guard to practice their rescue techniques. Unusual events such as these will probably generate more enthusiasm and participation than a spaghetti supper ever could.

For any work project, consider these questions: How much money can be earned? Can we find a way to earn more money from this event? Almost any idea can make more money than is obvious. For example, if the youth want to have a car wash, let them sell tickets for a week or two before the event. Some people will donate money who never will have their cars washed. Others who normally would not have participated will come because they bought the ticket.

One youth group planned a bake sale—an event which could earn a minimal amount of money. To involve more people and to raise more money, the youth expanded the project in a number of ways. They held the bake sale at the end of the Wednesday evening meal. Baked goods were sold by the serving, and no dessert was served at the meal. No coffee was served with dinner, so those wanting coffee had to buy their coffee at the bake sale. The bake sale was also a contest. Persons who contributed desserts paid to enter the contest. Awards were given in various categories, and the price of the serving was determined by the award. First-place desserts cost the most, for example. Recipes were also sold. This group used an old idea in a novel way and earned considerably more money.

Discover Creative Methods of Financing the Youth Ministry

Most church budgets won't cover all a youth group's expenses, and fund-raising is not the solution for all financial needs. The youth retreat may cost only $20, but a family with two teenagers may not have $40 to spend on a retreat. The youth ministry coordinator needs to be sensitive to persons who cannot afford even after-church pizza. The solution is not to delete youth activities but to find ways to include all youth without embarrassing them or calling attention to their need.

In addition to youth who need extra help to participate in youth ministry activities are the sponsoring adults. Many times the same adults accompany youth on nearly all of their outings. And many times adults leaders are single young adults; parents who are also paying for their youth's expenses; or senior adults on a fixed income. Some consideration should be made for the expenses of adult leaders. Although many adults will refuse the financial help, offering to pay the expenses of adults shows thoughtfulness and appreciation for those dependable adults. And if the offer is routinely made, those adults who do need the help can more comfortably accept it.

This also applies to the youth ministry coordinator. The youth leader, whether volunteer, part-time, or full-time, participates in all youth activities. Sometimes the expense is more than any personal budget can bear. A church certainly needs to provide an expense account for the youth ministry coordinator.

A church likely can discover a variety of ways to subsidize youth ministry. A few suggestions are:

• Include some money in the budget for this kind of expenditure.

• Provide a way for adults who are interested in the youth ministry, but who cannot physically participate, to contribute financial support.

• Consider a scholarship approach for major events.
• Help youth find part-time work to earn money for church activities.
• Take advantage of fast-food restaurants and motels that provide free food and services for bus drivers and/or adults leaders.

A youth ministry coordinator will work with many kinds of resources—people, facilities, materials, furnishings, and money. With good planning and some creativity all of these resources can be used appropriately and wisely to give the youth ministry balance, challenge, and excitement. Young lives are far more important than dollars, but how dollars are spent can impact how much ministry is accomplished. Give financial planning all the importance and attention it deserves, but make dollars a tool for ministry!

Personal Learning Activities

1. What five elements should be considered for each line item of a proposed budget?

2. Describe a process you can use in proposing a youth ministry budget for your church.

3. For what reasons might a youth group consider fundraising?

4. For whom should a church consider helping with expenses?

Chapter Nine

Planning Great Activities for Small Churches

Richard Ross

Richard Ross is youth ministry consultant, Church Administration Department, Sunday School Board, Nashville, Tennessee.

Adopt a Grandparent

The need.—Youth tend to focus exclusively on their own age group. Senior adults wonder if younger church members genuinely care about them. Both generations possess qualities that could be valuable to the other.

The idea.—Youth leaders pair youth and senior adults who want to participate. The first Sunday of the emphasis youth and their adopted grandparents sit together in worship. The second Sunday the youth bring the senior adults a greeting card or simple gift. The third Sunday the youth visit in the senior adults' homes. The fourth Sunday the total group participates in a noon luncheon at church. The luncheon includes testimonies about the ways new friendships have blessed lives.

In small churches.—This plan works well with even one youth and one senior adult. With a small number of pairs, the luncheon on the fourth Sunday could be held in a home.

Planning resource.—Richard Ross, compiler, *Successes in Southern Baptist Youth Ministry* (Nashville: Convention, 1988), 109, 126.

After-Game Fellowship

The need.—Youth need positive alternatives to unhealthy social events which frequently follow football games. Also youth need well-planned events to which they can invite their unchurched friends. Youth need informal events which help them feel closer to the other youth and their leaders.

The idea.—Youth and leaders plan a social event to follow an in-town football game. The event may be held at the church, a home, or commercial facility (restaurant), etc. The event usually includes time for planned activities and time for youth to visit informally. It may include a video replay of game highlights, halftime entertainment, and youth in the stands. The event may include a creative, low-key presentation of the plan of salvation.

In small churches.—With small groups most of the youth need to attend or the event will seem like a failure. All youth need to be invovled in planning and preparing for the fellowship in order to guarantee their participation. Also ask the youth group, "What do we need to do in planning this fellowship to make you feel good about inviting your unchurched friends?"

Choose a location for the fellowship appropriate for the anticipated attendance. Feeling crowded in a living room or a small restaurant room is better than feeling lost in a large area.

Planning resources.—Richard Ross, compiler, *Youth Ministry Planbook 4* (Nashville: Convention, 1989), 37. Frank Hart Smith, compiler, *52 Complete After Game Fellowships* (Nashville: Convention, 1980).

Baptist Doctrine Study

The need.—Many teenagers do not know in Christian doctrine. This includes new Christians, youth just beginning to attend church, youth who grew up in other denominations, youth in homes with little or no religious instruction, and youth who are just becoming interested in affirming a personal belief system.

The idea.—Youth meet several times one week or once a week for several weeks in April. Youth study a different doctrine each year. Sessions are held at church, in homes, or some other location.

In small churches.—In small youth groups, every teenager can help prepare for this study. Some can work on publicity; others can make the meeting room visually interesting. Still others can bring refreshments or help guide learning activities. Broad involvement strengthens attendance.

Planning resources.—The current Baptist Doctrine study book for youth. Richard Ross, compiler, *Youth Ministry Planbook 4* (Nashville: Convention, 1989), 39.

Conference Center Trip
The need.—Youth need the spiritual and emotional bonding that out-of-town trips can provide. They need to spend time with gifted teachers, leaders, and Christian artists. They need to build friendships with Christian peer role models.

The idea.—Youth and their sponsors travel in the summer to Glorieta, New Mexico, or Ridgecrest, North Carolina, for a conference lasting about seven days. Youth may attend such weeks as Centrifuge, Summer Youth Celebration, Church Recreation Week, Music Week, or a week related to missions. Centrifuge is also offered on selected Baptist college campuses and in selected state camps. Ski Bible conferences and Winter Weekends are provided during the winter months.

In small churches.—Teenagers in smaller churches may sometimes feel that not many youth are Christians. A week spent with several hundred Christian youth at a conference center can be a genuine spiritual boost.

In such large groups youth from small churches can build friendships with other youth with similar personalities and interests. Such friendships may be more limited at home. New friends can give each other insights about living the Christian Life.

Planning resources.—For a listing of conference events, write Ridgecrest Baptist Conference Center, P. O. Box 128,

Ridgecrest, NC 28770 or Glorieta Baptist Conference Center, P. O. Box 8, Glorieta, NM 87335. For information about Centrifuge, write Centrifuge, Church Recreation Department, Baptist Sunday School Board, 127 Ninth Avenue, North, Nashville, TN 37234. Richard Ross, compiler, *Summer Youth Ministry Ideas* (Nashville: Convention, 1985), 60-70. Richard Ross, compiler, *Youth Ministry Planbook 4* (Nashville: Convention, 1989), 43.

DiscipleNow Weekend
The need.—Youth need experiences that deepen their walk with God and bond the group together.

The idea.—Groups of youth spend the weekend living in church members' homes as families. Youth leaders live with each group and also lead discipleship experiences. The weekend includes times when for groups to come together at church, to go out for recreation, and to have Discipleship Training experiences in the host homes. These experiences usually focus on personal Bible study, daily quiet time, prayer, and sharing one's faith. Parents assist the host family by bringing in prepared food. Boys sleep in one area of the house and girls in another. "Families" attend church together on Sunday morning and come back on Sunday afternoon for debriefing. Some churches invite guests to lead in each home.

In small churches.—This plan works equally well even if only one house is needed. If more than 10 youth will be involved, provide one house for younger youth and one for older.

Planning resources.—R. Clyde Hall, Jr. and Wesley Black, compilers, *DiscipleNow Manual* (Nashville: Convention, 1985). Richard Ross, compiler, *Youth Ministry Planbook 4*, (Nashville: Convention, 1989), 44.

Fellowship Dinner
The need.—Youth need experiences which highlight their sense of belonging to the church and the youth group. Youth also need informal social contact with members of the opposite sex in order to learn relationship skills.

The idea.—Youth and leaders plan a dinner celebrating friendships within the youth group. The dinner can be held any time during the year. Some churches may plan it in February. The dinner can be held at church or away. Youth may bring a friend of the opposite sex to the banquet, but this is neither required nor highlighted. Youth profit most from the event when they are directly involved in preparing for it. Youth help with publicity, financing, menu, decorations, entertainment, and cleanup. Youth leaders and parents assist but keep youth in the forefront of preparations.

In small churches.—Small youth groups might enjoy holding the dinner in a comfortable home. Such a setting might be preferable to a small group meeting in a large room at church. Also the term *dinner* may seem less intimidating than *banquet* to a small group.

Planning resources.—Richard Ross, compiler, *Summer Youth Ministry Ideas* (Nashville: Convention, 1985), 77-86. Richard Ross, compiler, *Youth Ministry Planbook 4* (Nashville: Convention, 1989), 38. Ewilda Fancher, *Social Recreation as Ministry* (Nashville: Convention, 1989). Richard Ross, compiler, *Successes in Southern Baptist Youth Ministry* (Nashville: Convention, 1988), 84.

January Bible Study
The need.—Youth need periods of intensive Bible study. Youth often need a spiritual lift in the dead of winter.

The idea.—Youth meet several times in January to give intensive study to one book of the Bible. Most groups meet several evenings one week. Other groups meet once a week for several weeks. Study may be at the church, in homes, or other creative locations, such as studying the prison epistles in a jail cell.

In small churches.—Consider tying the study to a progressive supper. Cover one session of the study at each stop. Consider using the pastor, other staff members, or church leaders as teachers in order to expose youth to fresh teaching approaches.

Planning resources.—*January Bible Study Planning Package.* Richard Ross, compiler, *Youth Ministry Planbook 4* (Nashville: Convention, 1989), 46.

Life Commitment Weekend
The need.—Finding God's will concerning vocation is a significant developmental issue for Christian youth. Youth need to acknowledge God's leadership in this area of life. They need to express an openness to a call to church-related vocations. They also need to examine secular vocations to which God could lead.

The idea.—Youth and leaders plan a weekend to give special emphasis to vocational direction and total life commitment. The weekend can be held anytime, or it can be planned in April as suggested on the denominational calendar. The weekend may include special sermons, testimonies, and music on life commitment in the worship services; a youth group meeting for adults representing a variety of vocations to share about their work; a time for staff members to share with youth how they heard God's call; or a special invitation of appeal to life commitment.

In small churches.—In the summer or during a school break, some adults may be willing to take youth to their workplace for a day or a half-day. This gives youth new insights into vocations in which they may have an interest. Staff ministers may be willing to allow a youth to shadow them for a day, too.

Planning resource.—Richard Ross, compiler, *Youth Ministry Planbook 4* (Nashville: Convention, 1989), 48.

Local Mission Action Project

The need.—Youth need to reach out beyond the four walls of the church. They need to meet the spiritual, physical, and emotional needs of diverse groups. Youth need concrete experiences that help them to feel better about themselves and to sense they can make a difference in the world.

The idea.—Ideally mission action projects are coordinated by the youth missions education organizations—Acteens, Pioneer Royal Ambassadors, and High School Baptist Young Men. The leaders guide the youth to choose a need in the local area they can help meet. Most mission action projects are designed to benefit an identifiable group, such as the economically disadvantaged, illiterate, elderly, hospitalized, or handicapped.

The project chosen depends on local needs, the size and abilities of the youth group, time available, and response of the youth. Teenagers usually study and prepare for the project during the regular meeting times for their missions organizations.

In small churches.—Groups as small as two can and should participate in mission action projects. Every community and rural area has needs small groups of youth can meet. The key is to choose projects that can be successfully completed by the youth available.

Planning resource.—Richard Ross, compiler, *Summer Youth*

Ministry Ideas (Nashville: Convention, 1985), 54-62.

Mission Trip

The need.—Youth need intensive mission experiences that give them time to develop significant relationships with people in need. Youth need a break from their at-home routine in order to hear the voice of God in fresh ways and to concentrate on deepening relationships with Christian peers.

The idea.—Youth spend 5-10 days away from home meeting needs with an identifiable group of people. Ideally, the youth missions education organizations provide preparation for the trip. Additional staff members, parents, or sponsors may accompany the group.

In small churches.—Leaders who want youth groups to travel to help them often prefer small groups. These pastors, missionaries, and Christian social workers, have found small groups to be less of a burden logistically and just as prepared.

Large church budgets often include hundreds or thousands of dollars for mission trips. Smaller churches without these resources should give careful thought to financing. Youth leaders should ask the church to clarify the church's position regarding fund-raising, scholarships, and budget support.

Planning resources.—Valerie Hardy and R. Clyde Hall, compilers, *Mission Trip Administrative Manual, Revised* (Nashville: Convention Press,). Richard Ross, compiler, *Youth Ministry Planbook 4* (Nashville: Convention, 1989), 51.

Mission Vacation Bible School

The need.—Youth need opportunities to share their faith in Christ with others. Teenagers who struggle with self-esteem issues need the personal affirmation that comes from sacrificially giving to others. Youth need the goal of a mission project to motivate them to prepare and grow.

The idea.—Youth lead a weeklong Vacation Bible School away from their own church. The school may be local or in another city or state. The school may involve children of other races or children who are economically disadvantaged. The school may also be targeted to children living in an area with no Baptist witness. Some schools include youth and even adults. The sponsoring youth may lead the school on their own, or they may work in partnership with local leaders.

In small churches.—Smaller youth groups can lead a quality mission VBS for an appropriate number of children. Or they can teach alongside adults from their church or with adults and youth from the area they are serving.

Small youth groups have the advantage of not overwhelming the area they are serving. Small youth groups are also easier to care for logistically if the mission VBS is conducted out of town.

Planning resources.—Mission VBS curriculum. *Backyard Bible Club/Mission VBS Director's Guide.* Richard Ross, compiler, *Youth Ministry Planbook 4* (Nashville: Convention, 1989), 52.

Outreach Bible Study

The need.—Some unchurched youth can be best reached by exposing them to Bible study away from the church buildings. Also active church youth need concrete ways to reach out to their lost friends.

The idea.—Youth and their leaders organize an eight-week Bible study away from the church. This weekly Bible study is designed for youth with little church background. Active youth bring lost friends to the full series of studies. At the end of the study, youth and leaders seek to involve prospects in ongoing Bible study groups at the church.

In small churches.—In small youth groups the entire group can participate in an Outreach Bible Study. Each teenager can involve one or more lost friends.

Planning resources.—Harry Piland, compiler, *How to Conduct Outreach Bible Study* (Nashville: Convention, 1986). Richard Ross, compiler, *Youth Ministry Planbook 4* (Nashville: Convention, 1989), 53.

Parent and Youth Dialogue

The need.—Developmental issues facing both parents and youth make communication between the two a challenge. Youth and parents need structured experiences that give them help in this area.

The idea.—Leaders, parents, and youth plan an event to aid communication in families. Parents and youth meet together to learn better ways of expressing and hearing thoughts and feelings. The specific experiences chosen for a dialogue vary with the goals for the event. Selected parents and youth may serve

104

on a panel, responding to open-ended questions from the audience. Or participants may be placed in make-believe families for role plays or dialogue. Many other variations are possible.

In small churches.—As few as five youth and five adults can enjoy a parent and youth dialogue. Rather than selecting a panel, allow all the members of one generation to respond to written questions from the other generation. Examples: How should we parents respond when a youth's grades begin to drop without reason? How can we get parents to trust us again after we have messed up one time?

Planning resources.—Richard Ross and Wade Rowatt, compilers, *Ministry with Youth and Their Parents* (Nashville: Convention, 1986), 115-18. Richard Ross, compiler, *Youth Ministry Planbook 4* (Nashville: Convention), 57.

Parent and Youth Double Date

The need.—Youth and parents need experiences which deepen communication, strengthen relationships, and provide relief from daily stress.

The idea.—Youth couples schedule two double dates with their parents. The youth plan one date, and the parents plan the other. Each generation tries to plan a date the other would enjoy. Youth couples don't have to be dating steadily; they can just be good friends. All participants gather for a fellowship after the dates to share stories and insights learned.

In small churches.—Encourage youth of dating age to find Christian friends in other churches to be their dates.

Planning resource.—Richard Ross, compiler, *Successes in Southern Baptist Youth Ministry* (Nashville: Convention, 1988), 11.

Parent Appreciation Dinner

The need.—Youth tend to forget to express appreciation to parents. Some youth feel guilty because they tend to take parents for granted. Teenagers need ways to express appreciation tangibly. Parents struggling with the stress of child rearing need positive, affirming experiences with their teenagers.

The idea.—Youth plan a special dinner for their parents, including parents who do not attend church. Committees of youth and leaders plan publicity, room and table decorations, food, and entertainment. A theme can help tie these elements together. Youth purchase inexpensive tickets to give to their parents. Income from ticket sales helps pay for the food and decorations. Entertainment might feature music, skits, brief speeches about the value of parents, or game-show activities.

In small churches.—Churches with fewer than seven or eight youth families might consider having the dinner in a home.

Planning resources.—Richard Ross and Wade Rowatt, compilers, *Ministry with Youth and Their Parents* (Nashville: Convention Press, 1986), 108-10. Richard Ross, compiler, *Youth Ministry Planbook 4* (Nashville: Convention Press, 1989), 55.

Youth Ministry Survey

The need.—Staff ministers, youth leaders, and Youth Ministry Council members need accurate data concerning needs in order to plan effectively.

The idea.—Leaders administer the Shared Ministry Survey to youth, youth parents, and youth workers. The pencil-and-paper survey takes approximately 20 minutes to complete. The groups surveyed evaluate many elements of youth ministry in the church, noting both strengthens and weaknesses. After the anonymous forms are collected, several leaders consolidate the responses and graph the data on large wall charts. By graphing youth, parents, and workers separately, interesting comparisons can be made. Those who guide the youth program will quickly identify strengths that can be built upon and needs that should be positively addressed. The result is a youth calendar based on reality rather than guesses.

In small churches.—Leaders can survey almost all youth, parents, and workers in smaller churches. This produces data that is highly reliable. In small churches all of these groups may want to meet together for discussion and planning after the surveys are tabulated and graphed.

Planning resource.—Order the free brochure "Shared Ministry Youth Survey" available by writing the Church Staff Support Section, 127 Ninth Avenue, North, Nashville, TN 37234.

Youth Vacation Bible School

The need.—Youth need intensive periods of Bible study in an informal, creative environment.

The idea.—Youth meet for Bible study and related activities 5 or 10 weekdays in a row in the summer. Meetings may run concurrently with children's VBS or be held different weeks. Meetings can be morning, afternoon, or evening. The group may meet at church, in homes, or outdoors. Youth usually have one, two, or three study periods each meeting. These study periods correspond to different units of study. Many youth groups also include creative recreation in the daily schedule.

In small churches.—Many small churches need youth to help staff a VBS for children. In those churches planning Youth VBS for other weeks is usually better.

Planning resources.—Current Youth VBS materials. Richard Ross, compiler, *Youth Ministry Planbook 4* (Nashville: Convention, 1989), 65.

Youth Week

The need.—Youth need to experience various leadership roles in the church. Youth need to feel that they are a vital part of the church today, not just in the future. Adults need to see teenagers taking active roles in the church.

The idea.—Youth accept church leadership roles for a week or a weekend. Youth volunteer to teach as many Sunday School classes as possible the final Sunday morning. Youth may also serve as church staff members for the week. For example, a young person serving as Youth Week pastor might accompany the church pastor as he makes hospital visits or contacts prospects. Youth may also serve as deacons, committee members, or other leaders. Youth Week usually climaxes with teenagers' leading a Sunday morning or evening worship service.

In small churches.—Youth Week can be effective regardless of how many positions youth fill. For example, youth do not have to teach every Sunday School class or fill every staff position. The goal is to allow youth who do want to serve to have that privilege.

Youth leaders should help ensure that teenagers are not embarrassed about their work during Youth Week. Leaders should offer to help individual youth prepare for their responsibilities.

Planning resources.—Jonathan Pedersen, compiler, *Youth Week Idea Pack* (Nashville: Convention, 1984). Richard Ross, compiler, *Youth Ministry Planbook 4* (Nashville: Convention, 1989), 66.

Briefly Noted

Here are several other creative ideas.

Christian music tape library.—The church or youth group provides funds to purchase contemporary Christian music tapes which can be checked out to youth. See Richard Ross, compiler, *Successes in Southern Baptist Youth Ministry* (Nashville: Convention, 1988), 119-20.

Lockin.—Youth spend a night in recreation and spiritual growth. See Richard Ross, compiler, *Youth Ministry Planbook 4* (Nashville: Convention, 1989), 49.

Night out for parents.—Youth provide babysitting at church for parents wanting a night out. See Richard Ross, compiler, *Successes in Southern Baptist Youth Ministry* (Nashville: Convention, 1988), 122-23.

Road rally.—Carloads of youth with adult drivers cover a preselected course searching for clues hidden at people-serving agencies. See Richard Ross, compiler, *Successes in Southern Baptist Youth Ministry* (Nashville: Convention, 1988), 105-107.

Snow ski trip.—Daytime skiing and evening Bible studies and sharing. See Richard Ross, compiler, *Youth Ministry Planbook 4* (Nashville: Convention, 1989), 61.

Warm, fuzzy line.—Ongoing way for youth and leaders to write affirming notes to one another. See Richard Ross, compiler, *Successes in Southern Baptist Youth Ministry* (Nashville: Convention, 1988), 62-63.

WOW Event.—Youth meet for specific help in sharing their faith. See *WOW Event Leader's Guide* (HMB); Richard Ross, compiler, *Youth Ministry Planbook 4* (Nashville: Convention, 1989), 63.

Youth flower ministry.—Youth meet Monday after school to separate pulpit flowers into small arrangements for delivery to shut-ins, etc. See Richard Ross, compiler, *Successes in Southern Baptist Youth Ministry* (Nashville: Convention, 1988), 74-75.

Personal Learning Activities

1. Choose three activities for your youth group. What needs do they meet for your youth and your church?

Chapter Ten

Reaching Out—Small Youth Groups That Don't Stay Small

Tony Rodgers

Tony Rodgers is minister of youth, First Baptist Church, Soddy Daisy, Tennessee.

Many years ago when I was a teenager, a Wednesday night message delivered by my pastor, Howard (Jakie) Carmicle, Jr. changed my life. As I took my seat near the back of the sanctuary, I thought this would be just another ordinary midweek service. Unknown to me, God had a specific purpose for my presence therethat night. Immediately I was absorbed in what the pastor was saying. I remember his saying that every person in the church has a task to do and how this church, my home church in rural central Kentucky, needs every person to fulfill his or her task so that our church could be the kind of church God intended it to be. I knew I was not doing all that God had intended for me to do.

As the invitation hymn began, I nearly jumped into the aisle and moved quickly to take my pastor's hand. When he asked me why I had come, I looked him squarely in the eyes and said, "Bro. Jakie, if anything in this church needs to be done, from sweeping the floors to preaching, I'll do it!" That night I didn't know all the blessings God had in store for me, but I knew I wanted to be exactly what He wanted me to be.

Just as God called me that night, God wants to use you right where you are to reach teenagers in your community. Every youth group should have a purpose, a goal, a dream, a vision. Proverbs 29:18 states: "Where there is no vision, the people perish." A ship without a rudder is doomed before it ever sets sail. In the same way, if you design, create, plan, and promote without first deciding why you are doing all of this, your efforts are doomed from the start.

If you are going to be involved in the lives of teenagers in your church and community, you must first determine the purpose for your involvement. Just as God has called you, one primary purpose of youth ministry in your church is to lead teenagers to be active in God's business. Herein lies the secret for small youth groups that do not remain small.

Evangelism is the work of God redeeming His creation in Jesus Christ. The youth group that reaches out to those in the community around it is participating in God's mission. Hal Poe, in *Handbook for Youth Evangelism*, spells out the need for this kind of purpose:

> In order for the group to be evangelistic, it must be open to outsiders. The members of the group must see themselves as the evangelists. An effective ministry of youth evangelism depends upon the desire of the Christians in the group to want others to know Christ as personal Savior. This desire runs counter to the natural youth tendency to have an exclusive group, but through a consciously planned program of study and ministry the exclusiveness can change to openness. Focusing on Christ instead of on itself will help a youth group remain open. Though youth have deep needs, the focus of youth ministry should not be on the need, but on how Christ answers the need.[1]

Witnessing to others is the responsibility of every Christian. Whether your group consists of 5 or 50, you have unlimited potential in God's work of redemption. Whatever the size of your group, the responsibility is the same.

You are already structured for effective ministry. Research repeatedly verifies that small groups attract and assimilate new members more quickly and effectively than do larger ones. That is why a healthy Sunday School organization uses the mathematical process of divide and multiply. The idea is that once a class becomes so large the teacher cannot have a personal relationship with each class member the class should be divided. Assuming both classes continue ministering and reaching as the first class did, soon those two classes will have multiplied the members and are again ready to divide to allow for more members.

In small churches individual, one-to-one relationships are more likely to develop between 5-10 youth than with 40-50. Getting to know youth personally in a small group is a privilege for the youth ministry coordinator. And working with these youth is also a challenge and an opportunity to influence them to likewise become involved in the lives of other teenagers in the community.

Let's take a look at five basic youth evangelism strategies based on Christ's life and ministry. Just as we see a variety of approaches practiced in Christ's ministry, so we too should be prepared to use several different approaches in reaching persons for Christ.

Prayer

As we look in the Scriptures, we see many instances when Jesus spent time in prayer before ministering to people or prior to making important decisions regarding individuals. Prayer must precede our efforts of sharing the good news with those we seek to win. "You can do more than pray, after you have prayed. But you can do no more than pray until you have prayed!"[2] Jesus prayed before He preached and ministered to people (see Mark 1:35-39). He prayed before He chose the twelve (see Luke 6:12). And He prayed before He went into the garden of Gethsemane prior to His crucifixion (see John 17:1-26). Jesus modeled prayer for us. He prayed throughout his ministry. Shouldn't we then also pray? We must pray for spiritual awakening in the lives of the lost and for guidance and help as we try to share the good news of Christ. If you can say with John Wesley that "God will do nothing but in answer to prayer,"[3] you have grasped the importance of prayer to an active ministry.

Keep a prayer list; and record the date of the request, the specific request, names, and the answer. These records of answered prayers will illustrate how God is working in the lives of your youth.

Relational Evangelism

The second approach Jesus used is sometimes called relational evangelism. This approach is based on Christians forming personal relationships with others.

This approach operates on multiple levels. For example, when you minister to one of your close friends, your influence not only affects your friend but can also pass through her to one or more of her friends. You can actually minister to other people as you minister to and through your friend.

We see one example of relational evangelism from Jesus' ministry as He ministered to the Gadarenes demoniac. Jesus' ministry affected the entire city (see Luke 8:39). Then John 1:40-51 records two instances of Jesus' calling a person to follow Him who immediately brought another to the Master.

Another clear picture of how ministering to one person can affect a whole group is seen in Jesus' ministry to the Samaritan woman at the well. "And from that city many of the Samaritans believed in Him because of the word of the woman who testified (John 4:39, NASB).[4] Jesus often practiced relational evangelism, and His ministry to one person influenced other persons or groups.

Experience affirms this kind of evangelism. The story is repeated daily. Parents once again become active in the local church after removing their support because of an incident that occurred years ago. The reason for the reinstatement is an active youth group that ministered to the needs of their teenager. A family joins the church after sporadic attendance in another denomination because their daughter began attending and was ministered to by an accepting and caring youth group.

Relational evangelism could be pictured as ripples on water caused by a pebble. Although the pebble makes contact at only one point on the water's surface, the ripples extend far from the original point of contact. This kind of evangelism can quickly multiply. To illustrate, suppose you set out to win 10,000 people to the Lord. If you won one person to Christ every day, you would need 28 years to reach your goal. But, if you won one every day and each of those also won one person to Christ every day from the day of their conversion, 16,000 could be led to the Lord in only two weeks!

One effective strategy for accomplishing relational evangelism is the LifeStyle meetings which are part of DiscipleYouth II. These meetings are led by two youth who have been through DiscipleYouth I and II or who have otherwise been trained to witness to peers about Jesus Christ.

The meeting might start anytime during the afternoon or evening, but beginning it after the evening meal works well. The meeting generally takes place in a youth's home. The host family plans music (contemporary Christian or theme related) and provides refreshments. Another youth is responsible for mixers (about 10-15 minutes of icebreakers as youth arrive) and the message. Youth invite lost friends to a great time of fellowship. An accompanying lost youth is the admission ticket to the LifeStyle meeting.

Ideas and handouts on the LifeStyle message can be found in the *DiscipleYouth II Notebook* or in issues of *equipping youth* magazine. After about 10-15 minutes of discussion centered around the message, refreshments are served. During this time the trained youth talk with the guests about the message and look for opportunities to witness. After 20-30 minutes of fellowship, the LifeStyle meeting is adjourned.

The effectiveness of LifeStyle meetings depends on the relationships Christian youth have with those outside the faith. Youth should be made aware that this kind of relationship usually takes time. They should be encouraged to cultivate new friendships not only for the purpose of gaining new friends but also for sharing their faith.[5]

The LifeStyle meeting is by no means the only expression of relational evangelism. Basically any service form of ministry can be the basis for a relationship. Plan for youth to help some elderly persons in your community go grocery shopping or have the youth shop for them. With any encouragement at all, relationships will develop.

On a hot summer day, on the day of the big parade, or during a walkathon, provide free cups of ice water on a main street, on the town square, or wherever people get hot and thirsty. A positive impression will result, and relationships will be started.

Free car washes for the people of your community will promote many new relationships. Relational evangelism takes the opportunity to use these relationships as a means for sharing Christ.

Environmental Evangelism

The third approach Jesus used to evangelize the lost is called environmental evangelism. Jesus was the master of telling parables which related spiritual truths to a present situation. Jesus seized the teachable moment when the woman came to the well for water and Jesus told her about "living water" (John 4:11). Jesus spoke to those who were farmers about sowing seeds of truth (see Matt. 13:24-30). He spoke about a person's influence by referring to leaven and bread (see Matt. 13:36-50). He taught the importance of the individual in God's eyes as He spoke of the one lost sheep which the shepherd would leave the 99 to find (see Luke 15).

Environmental evangelism puts the good news of Christ in the everyday language of the hearers. Youth should be trained to open their eyes and see what interests surround a lost person.

Suppose you meet a youth at the local library. You may want to talk about the greatest story ever told or about the greatest Book ever written. To the youth who says he's going fishing next Friday, you may want to talk about being a fisher of men. With a youth who is regularly wearing shiny black boots and army fatigues, you might talk about the battles in life.

Environmental evangelism may include approaches other than conversation. You can videotape a youth musical, a high-school ball game, or a community celebration and show it on a large-screen TV at the local pizza place (with the owner's permission, of course). Youth who are interested in and talented in electronics can help plan this event. Besides reaching the community, you may develop a relationship and involve a youth who has previously been on the fringe of the group.

Whatever event you sponsor, be sure to have trained youth and adults on hand to present the gospel wherever the opportunity arises. Creativity allows this approach to provide variety, enthusiasm, and social action outside the walls of the church.

Through participation in this kind of evangelism, Christian youth will realize that their faith is to be woven into their everyday lives.

Presentational Evangelism

Presentational evangelism is the kind of personal confrontation that frightens many Christian youth. Door-to-door witnessing is included in this category, but so are many other, less threatening methods. Community surveys, Bible distributions, and evangelism rallies are also forms of this approach to evangelism. In each case youth can present the gospel or provide a ministry. In fact, a bowling party, an after-church fellowship, or a Sunday School class hayride can all be presentational evangelism if the event is planned for the purpose of sharing Christ.

Youth are great procrastinators, and many will continue to put off witnessing. Christian youth need training in how to witness. Then they need planned opportunity. As they practice what they have been trained to do, they will know the joy of sharing their faith, they will be more certain of their own faith, and they will develop for a lifetime of sharing their faith with others.

A youth can maintain a Christian life-style in the world right in front of a lost person, but that person needs to hear the gospel message in order to accept Christ as Lord and Savior. If youth are too afraid to make the presentation themselves, challenge them to bring their friends to you. This is a starting point in their witnessing. Every time Christian youth see you present the gospel, they will grow in their courage until eventually they feel comfortable sharing themselves.

Informational Evangelism

Jesus was often surrounded by a crowd—10 lepers (see Luke 17:12) or 5,000 or more (see Matt. 14:15-21). At these times Jesus "sought to redeem all who would come to Him."[6]

From the Bible as well as from the life of Christ, we realize that God's desire is that all would come to believe in His Son. We are responsible to do all we can to tell the good news to everyone. This approach may be seen in media as varied as T-shirts with Christian messages, bumper stickers, and television programming.

This approach may seem rather indirect, but it needs to be taken seriously. It can be effectively used by youth, but it can also be misused. If misused, this approach can damage a person's or a church's witness. For example, a youth who misbehaves while wearing a Christian T-shirt may unintentionally give the wrong witness. Or a youth in a T-shirt with a Christian message who cannot cannot explain its meaning may make the good news seem frivolous. Other misuses may occur if a church's bumper sticker is seen on the back of a car that is sitting at the local liquor store or a carful of youth that is being driven wrecklessly.

The goal of this kind of evangelism is not to get youth to try to act religious all the time but to understand the need of the lost world and that they can help meet that need in a variety of ways.

As Christians we are to go everywhere with the good news of Christ. We are to equip new Christians so that they too can bear fruit. We are to go with the gospel to our neighbors, the store clerk, the paper carrier, the youth who mows the yard, and the one who babysits our children.

We will fulfill the Great Commission by leading one person to Christ at a time. And we will lead these persons to Christ when we apply Jesus' methods of reaching people to our daily lives.

White Heart, a contemporary Christian music group, has a song entitled "We Are His Hands," and until we realize the truth behind these words, we will never really be serious about reaching one single person for Christ.

---

[1]Hal Poe, "A Theology of Youth Evangelism," in Dean Finley, compiler, *Handbook for Youth Evangelism* (Nashville: Broadman Press, 1988), 45.

[2]Ralph W. Neighbor, Jr. *Survival Kit I, Youth Edition* (Nashville: Convention Press, 1981), 55.

[3]As quoted in, Avery T. Willis, Jr., *The Biblical Basis of Missions* (Nashville: Convention Press, 1979), 142.

[4]From the *New American Standard Bible*. ©The Lockman Foundation, 1960, 1962, 1963, 1968, 1971, 1973, 1975, 1977. Used by persmission.

[5]For a more detailed explanation of the LifeStyle meeting, see , *Disciple Youth II Leaders Guide* (Nashville: Convention Press, 1985, 94-106; , *Disciple Youth II Notebook* (Nashville: Convention Press, 1985), 169-206; and various issues of *equipping youth.*

[6]Finley, 45.

Chapter Eleven

Accessing Denominational Support

Richard Ross

Richard Ross is youth ministry consultant, Church Administration Department, Sunday School Board, Nashville, Tennessee.

Youth leaders in small churches are on the front lines of a battle. Weekly they confront the negative influences that can harm teenagers. They relate to youth right in the trenches of home, school, church, and community.

Serving on the front lines is always a challenge. Most small church youth leaders struggle with genuine time limitations. Most experience stress as they battle a youth culture that continues to deteriorate. The majority are frustrated at limited budget support or an inadequate number of youth workers.

Front-line troops are crucial in any battle. Any wise general knows they must have support. Front-line Southern Baptist youth leaders have a support network that is without parallel.

Cooperation and mutual support have been hallmarks of Southern Baptist life. Youth leaders can continue the tradition of supporting others and receiving support. The association, state convention, and Southern Baptist Convention offer support for youth ministry.

The Association

A Baptist association can offer support to youth ministries in all sizes of churches. It can be of special help to small churches.

The association provides a way for youth, workers, and parents in small churches to have experiences they would otherwise miss. For example, many churches can cooperate to plan, finance, staff, and conduct a quality youth camp experience. Such a week would be impossible for small churches working alone.

Other associational projects that might be difficult for some small churches include:

- vocational guidance fair
- on-to-college rally
- weekend retreat
- amusement park event
- youth rally
- associational youth choir musical
- major local mission project
- mission trip
- senior graduation event
- Christian concert
- youth crusade
- parent appreciation banquet
- parenting seminar
- parent and youth retreat

Associational youth ministry projects can be a genuine help to small church youth leaders.

Those projects may generate new enthusiasm among youth because of the involvement with a larger group of teenagers.—A crowd attracts a crowd.

Associational projects can help with time limitations.—Even full-time, paid youth ministers experience time frustrations. Part-time, combination, and especially volunteer leaders continually struggle with too little time available.

Youth leaders who work together are able to produce a quality associational event in far less time than when working alone. Their teenagers are the direct beneficiaries.

Associational projects can help with financial limitations.— Youth leaders in some small churches must provide a youth program on a limited budget. Covering the expense of a Christian concert or a guest speaker may be unrealistic. Associational churches that pool their resources can make such programming possible.

Associational projects expose youth to other Christian teenagers.—Youth from small churches need to be reminded that significant numbers of teenagers share their faith. Fellowshiping at associational events can help youth from the same schools support one another in Christian living on campus.

The ministry of the association is dependent on the contribution church leaders make to it. Youth leaders who contribute their time and expertise to planning associational events make a genuine contribution to youth. Taking a turn serving as associational youth ministry coordinator (formerly called associational youth director) also opens new doors of service. (For a job description of an associational youth ministry coordinator, write to Richard Ross, 127 Ninth Avenue, North, Nashville, TN 37234.)

Most associations have offices with resources that can support youth ministry. Some stock audiovisual materials and equipment, books, and pamphlets which are available to churches at no cost. Your pastor can give you the phone numbers you need to check out available equipment and resources.

Associations also provide training opportunities for youth leaders. Most of these training events are related to church organizations. Therefore, youth leaders will usually find conferences related to Youth Sunday School, Youth Discipleship Training, Acteens, Pioneer Royal Ambassadors, High School Baptist Young Men, and Youth Music. These training events usually include help in understanding youth, using curricula, choosing teaching approaches, and planning for personal ministry outside a class.

Conferences may also be offered in such vital support services as church recreation, family ministry, or media library. Call your associational office to make sure you are on the mailing list that will bring you notice about such events.

Most associations elect officers and committees to support work in churches. For example, most elect an associational Sunday School director or even additional ASSISTeam members. Such officers take the lead in providing associational training conferences, but they may also be willing to provide training at your church. They may be willing to do this especially if your association is so large geographically that traveling to general conferences isn't always practical.

A growing number of associations provide a regular fellowship meeting of youth ministers and youth ministry coordinators. Some groups meet weekly; some meet monthly or quarterly.

Some associations provide formal meetings, often tied to a regular pastors' conference. Other meetings are informal and may include a meal at a local restaurant. Such meetings may or may not be publicized well. Call the associational office to discover if a group is presently meeting.

Such fellowship meetings can be an asset to your ministry. Other local youth leaders can be a source of information concerning retreat facilities, recreation facilities, resource personnel, and creative ideas.

Such a group can also be a good emotional and spiritual support. Youth ministry is rewarding but also stressful. Every youth leader needs a support group. Such a group can be especially helpful during periods of church conflict or when a youth is facing a crisis.

If no group is meeting in your area, you may want to help begin one. The associational director of missions, moderator, or youth ministry coordinator can help you. If you serve in an area with few Southern Baptist churches, you may want to meet with youth leaders from other evangelical churches.

The State Convention
Almost all Southern Baptist churches are related to one of approximately 37 state conventions or 4 state fellowships. (State fellowships become conventions when they reach a certain total church membership or total number of churches.)

State conventions and fellowships provide yet another level of support for youth ministry in small churches. (For brevity, only the term *state conventions* will be used for the remainder of the chapter.) Many state conventions provide programming for youth that would be difficult for small churches to provide. Examples include state youth camps, assemblies, music festivals, missions conventions, youth evangelism conferences, and weeks featuring discipleship and evangelism training.

State conventions also provide training for adults who work with youth. Most states print calendars that list all of the training events available. A call or letter to the state convention office will bring you a current copy.

Many state convention leaders want to communicate regularly with youth leaders and volunteer youth ministry coordinators. By getting on their mailing lists, information will come to you directly rather than to the church in general. To get on the list, call the state office and ask the receptionist to connect you with the leader who relates to youth ministry.

Most state conventions also stock free youth-related materials. These materials are available by request in reasonable quantities. When you call or write, describe your needs and the kind of materials that would help. Your request might be similar to these:

● Do you have material that would help me know how to begin an Acteens group?

● Can you help me choose which curriculum line will be best for our Youth Sunday School?

● I have just heard about Youth Bible Drill and Speakers Tournament. Can you send me more information?

With sufficient notice state convention leaders can sometimes come to individual churches. They may be able to tie such a trip to an existing trip to your part of the state. All state leaders welcome your calls and letters concerning specific needs.

Southern Baptist Convention

The Southern Baptist Convention has created a number of boards, agencies, institutions, and commissions to support the local church. Most offer specific support for youth leaders.

Many of these organizations have full-time professionals who give all of their time to support youth leaders. This group of more than 50 represents more than all other denominations combined.

Denominational professionals can better support you if they can communicate with you by mail. Mailings alert you to training opportunities, resources, and youth ministry ideas. You can place your name on the Convention mailing list in two ways. First, write to: Youth Ministry Consultant, MSN 157A, Baptist Sunday School Board, 127 Ninth Avenue, North, Nashville, TN 37234. Include your name, church, mailing address, title, and whether you are paid or volunteer. Second, ask your church clerk to list you as minister of youth on the Uniform Church Letter. The UCL is a long report completed by most Southern Baptist churches at the end of summer. If you coordinate the youth program for your church, you should be listed as minister of youth even if you have another title or no title at all.

Completing these two steps will place you on the Convention youth ministry mailing list. However, you must be listed on the UCL each fall or your name will be dropped from the list.

Convention boards and agencies provide for youth leaders several hundred training events each year. Many of these events are free. Food or lodging costs may require a modest fee.

You may also call or write to request information about specific training you want. Here are several addresses and phone numbers to help you.

Baptist Sunday School Board
127 Ninth Avenue, North
Nashville, TN 37234
(615) 251-2000
Youth Sunday School, Youth Discipleship Training, Youth Music, Church Recreation, Vocational Guidance, Youth Ministry Coordination, Family Ministry.

Brotherhood Commission
1548 Poplar Avenue
Memphis, TN 38104
(901) 272-2461
Missions education and missions involvement for teenage boys and young men.

Christian Life Commission
901 Commerce Street, #550
Nashville, TN 37203
(615) 244-2495
Moral and ethical issues affecting youth and families.

Foreign Mission Board
P.O. Box 6767
Richmond, VA 23230
(804) 353-0151

Foreign mission support and short-term foreign mission involvement.

Home Mission Board
1350 Spring Street, Northwest
Atlanta, GA 30367-5601
(404) 898-7000

Youth evangelism; home mission support; and short-term, home-mission assignments.

Woman's Missionary Union
100 Missionary Ridge
Birmingham, AL 35242-5235
(205) 991-8100

Missions education and missions involvement for teenage girls and young women.

Many Convention organizations produce materials to support the work of youth leaders. Many program helps and brochures are free. Books and periodicals are available at a modest cost. You may call or write the numbers and addresses listed above to inquire about materials currently available.

A good selection of youth ministry materials is available at Baptist Book Stores. You may purchase materials while visiting a store or by ordering by phone or by mail.

You may order all materials produced by the Sunday School Board by calling toll-free 1-800-458-BSSB. This includes all Convention Press books, Broadman books and supplies, and all church literature. Materials can be charged to the church, to an individual, or to personal bank cards.

Southern Baptist youth leaders face many challenges in their work. But they have a host of folk working full-time to support their ministries.

Group Learning Activities

Chapters 1-3

1. Create a visual, listing the nine advantages of smaller youth groups described in chapter one. Ask the group to give each of the advantages one of the following designations:

- *A base hit.*—We occasionally experience this advantage.
- *A double hit.*—We experience this advantage fairly often.
- *A triple hit.*—We experience this advantage most of the time.
- *A home run.*—We believe this is one of the most significant advantages of belonging to a small youth group.

2. Ask the group to compare the role of a youth ministry coordinator to a professional baseball coach. (Examples: He drafts players. He trains them. He helps the team develop a strategy.)

3. Divide participants into five groups. Assign to each group one of the five youth organizations described in chapter 3. Ask each group to help a spokesperson prepare a five-minute speech on, "What Will Happen to Our Youth if You Cut Our Organization from the Team."

Chapters 4-5

1. Give each participant approximately 10 football helmet designs cut from construction paper. Ask them to write on each helmet the name of one existing youth worker in their church. On the remaining helmets, ask them to write the position on their teams that are now vacant.

2. Divide the group into three teams of talent scouts. Assign the groups one of three target audiences—young adults, senior

adults, and parents. Using the material in chapter 4 as background, ask the three groups to list advantages of using members of their assigned target audiences as youth leaders. Ask each group to choose a spokesperson to present their scouting reports to the entire group.

3. Distribute calendars you have secured from association and state convention offices that lists training opportunities for youth leaders.

4. Ask participants to prepare a team roster of adults presently working in the youth organizations who should serve on a Youth Ministry Council. Ask participants to list on a large piece of paper qualities they would look for in youth they want to draft for the Council.

Chapters 6-8

1. Write the six myths found in chapter 6 on paper basketball backboards. Assign six groups to review the material which clarifies each myth. Ask six spokespersons to shatter (tear) each backboard and then share why that myth is untrue.

2. List on the wall the parent ministry events described in chapter 6. Keeping their own churches in mind, ask participants to classify each event idea as a:

● *One-point shot.*—Something that would be helpful someday.

● *Two-point shot.*—Some that that definitely should be addressed in the coming year.

● *Three-point shot.*—Something of vital importance that should be planned right away.

3. Prepare the group for a three-on-three assignment. Divide the participants into groups of three. Give each group a card on which is written a common youth event, such as "retreat," "Youth VBS," or "mission trip." Ask each group to brainstorm three forms of publicity and three publicity audiences for their assigned event. Share responses.

4. Divide participants into three groups. Give a basketball to group one. Ask them to name a common need in youth ministry such as lack of outreach or troubled families. Ask the group to toss the basketball to group two. Ask group two to brainstorm quickly a youth event, activity, or emphasis that would help meet the need raised by group one. Then ask the group to pass the basketball to group three. Ask group three to estimate

quickly the amount of money, if any, that should be included in an annual youth budget to pay for the event chosen by group two. Repeat the process several times.

Chapters 9-11

1. Sketch and reproduce for participants a soccer scoreboard. Label one side of the scoreboard as "Youth Baptisms" and the other "Youth Enrollment." As a goal-setting activity, ask participants to write in the final score they would like to see at the end of the game (the coming year of youth ministry).

2. Place a chair at the front of the room. Ask a participant to sit in the chair as goalie. Ask the participant to describe briefly a current need in his/her youth group. Ask the group to kick numerous programming ideas to the goalie that could address the need. Use chapter 9 as a reference. Give additional participants opportunities to be goalies as time permits.

3. Before the session ask three participants to review one of the sections from chapter 11 on association, state, and SBC support. During the session conduct a role play taking place in a locker room immediately after a soccer game. Enlist a participant to be a TV reporter and one to be the star (youth leader) who just kicked the winning goal. As the skit begins, ask the star to acknowledge to the reporter the three teammates who made the goal possible. The reporter then asks the three teammates noted above to describe how they provided (denominational) support to the star.

The Church Study Course is a Southern Baptist education system designed to support the training efforts of local churches. It provides courses, recognition, record keeping, and regular reports for some 20,000 participating churches.

The Church Study Course is characterized by short courses ranging from 2½ to 10 hours in length. They may be studied individually or in groups. With more than 600 courses in 24 subject areas, it offers 130 diploma plans in all areas of church leadership and Christian growth.

Complete details about the Church Study Course system, courses available, and diplomas offered may be found in a current copy of the *Church Study Course Catalog*.

The Church Study Course system is jointly sponsored by many agencies within the Southern Baptist Convention.

How to Request Credit for This Course

This book is the text for course number 23-071 in the subject area Pastoral Ministries. This course is designed for five hours of group study.

Credit for this course may be obtained in two ways:

1. Read the book and attend class sessions. (If you are absent from one or more sessions, complete the "Personal Learning Activities" for the material missed.)

2. Read the book and complete the "Personal Learning Activities." (Written work should be submitted to an appropriate church leader.)

A request for credit may be made on Form 725 "Church Study Course Enrollment/Credit Request" and sent to the Awards Office, Sunday School Board, 127 Ninth Avenue, North, Nashville, Tennessee 37234. The form on the following page may be used to request credit. Enrollment in a diploma plan may also be made on Form 725.

Within three months of your completion of a course, confirmation of your credit will be sent to your church. A copy of your complete transcript will be sent to your church annually during the July-September quarter if you have completed a course during the previous 12 months.

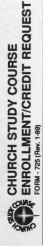

CHURCH STUDY COURSE
ENROLLMENT/CREDIT REQUEST
FORM - 725 (Rev. 1-89)

**MAIL THIS
REQUEST TO** ➤

CHURCH STUDY COURSE AWARDS OFFICE
BAPTIST SUNDAY SCHOOL BOARD
127 NINTH AVENUE, NORTH
NASHVILLE, TENNESSEE 37234

Is this the first course taken since 1983? ☐ **YES** If yes, or not sure complete all of Section 1. ☐ **NO** If no, complete only bold boxes in Section 1.

SECTION 1 - STUDENT I.D.

STUDENT

Social Security Number

☐ Mr. ☐ Miss
☐ Mrs.

Personal CSC Number* ➤

DATE OF BIRTH

Month	Day	Year

Name (First, MI, Last)

Street, Route, or P.O. Box

City, State   Zip Code

CHURCH

Church Name

Mailing Address

City, State   Zip Code

SECTION 2 - CHANGE REQUEST ONLY (Current inf. in Section 1)

☐ Former Name

☐ Former Address   Zip Code

☐ Former Church   Zip Code

SECTION 3 - COURSE CREDIT REQUEST

Course No.	Title (use exact title)
1. 23-071	*Big Help for Small Youth Groups*
2.	
3.	
4.	
5.	
6.	

SECTION 4 - DIPLOMA ENROLLMENT

Enter exact diploma title from current Church Study Course catalog. Indicate diploma age group if appropriate. Do not enroll again with each course. When all requirements have been met, the diploma will be mailed to your church. Enrollment in Christian Development Diplomas is automatic. No charge will be made for enrollment or diplomas.

☐ Title of Diploma	Age group or area
☐ Title of Diploma	Age group or area

Signature of Pastor, Teacher, or Other Church Leader	Date

*CSC # not required for new students. Others please give CSC # when using SS # for the first time. Then, only one ID # is required.